THE POWER OF *Positive* ENERGY

TANAAZ CHUBB
Creator of ForeverConscious.com

Everything You Need to Awaken Your Soul, Raise Your Vibration, and Manifest an Inspired Life

Adams Media
New York London Toronto Sydney New Delhi

adamsmedia
Adams Media
An Imprint of Simon & Schuster, Inc.
57 Littlefield Street
Avon, Massachusetts 02322

First Adams Media trade paperback edition AUGUST 2017

ADAMS MEDIA and colophon are trademarks of Simon and Schuster.

For information about special discounts for bulk purchases, please contact Simon & Schuster Special Sales at 1-866-506-1949 or business@simonandschuster.com.

The Simon & Schuster Speakers Bureau can bring authors to your live event. For more information or to book an event contact the Simon & Schuster Speakers Bureau at 1-866-248-3049 or visit our website at www.simonspeakers.com.

Interior design by Heather McKiel
Interior images © Getty Images

Manufactured in the United States of America

10 9 8 7 6 5 4 3

Library of Congress Cataloging-in-Publication Data has been applied for.

ISBN 978-1-5072-0253-1
ISBN 978-1-5072-0254-8 (ebook)

This book is intended as general information only, and should not be used to diagnose or treat any health condition. In light of the complex, individual, and specific nature of health problems, this book is not intended to replace professional medical advice. The ideas, procedures, and suggestions in this book are intended to supplement, not replace, the advice of a trained medical professional. Consult your physician before adopting any of the suggestions in this book, as well as about any condition that may require diagnosis or medical attention. The author and publisher disclaim any liability arising directly or indirectly from the use of this book.

DEDICATION

To my mother, who taught me the importance of good thoughts, good words, and good deeds.

CONTENTS

INTRODUCTION

Imagine being able to live a life that feels like it was created just for you. Imagine being able to live with ease and grace, secure in the knowledge that everything is unfolding exactly how it is meant to unfold. Imagine feeling so loved and so supported in your life every single day, that you have the confidence and the tools to go after your wildest dreams. All of this is possible with the power of positive energy.

Positive energy is so much more than just feeling happy and cheerful all the time. Positive energy is so much more than just putting a smile on your face and pretending that you don't have deeper thoughts and feelings. Positive energy is about attuning your life to the energetic vibration of your soul. It is about honoring the things that fill you up and make your entire body tingle and hum. It is about living from a place that is in harmony with your mind, your body, your soul, and the Universe.

Everything in this Universe carries an energetic vibration and when you tune in to these vibrations and align with the ones that feel good to you, the world becomes almost a magical place. Synchronicities appear, opportunities walk into your life as if by coincidence, the right people enter your life at the right time, and you feel the Universe responding to your every thought and feeling. When you sync your life with positive energy, this amazing world becomes your reality.

Perhaps deep inside you have already felt the rising of your soul, the stirring of energy in your being that has been calling on you to shift your life so that you can reach your fullest potential and live a life that feels joyful and purposeful. Perhaps you have even been drawn to this book as a reminder that you are a powerful being with the potential to create a life that feels positive, supportive, and loving, no matter what circumstances you find yourself in.

In this book, you are going to learn how to operate your life using positive energy. You will learn how to free yourself from negativity and fears and instead reconnect with your soul.

Through this connection, you will discover how to create a life that is filled with positive energy, not just temporarily but for the long term.

You are also going to learn how to open up to the magic inside of you and around you, so you can use it to find your purpose and align with a life that feels good from the inside out.

As you read this book, allow the words to inspire and guide you in whatever ways that feel right for you. It is best to read the book from start to finish, but there are no rules. As you read, be open to the idea that you are more than just a body—that you are a soul charged up with energy that is magical, powerful, and there for you to use. Being open to these possibilities allows you to connect with the life that was always meant for you.

So if you are ready to start living a positively inspired life that feels easy and joyous, then you have come to the right place. Let's get started.

PART 1

Learning to Embrace the Power of Your Energy

CHAPTER 1

AWAKENING TO YOURSELF AS AN ENERGETIC BEING

Dare to dream higher, dare to reach a little bit further, dare to step into your potential . . . for when you do, you will see that every day holds hundreds of opportunities that will rain down on you like glittering stars.

RECLAIMING YOUR POWER

Many of us forget that we have the power to shape our reality. Many of us forget that we have the ability to live life from a place that is so magical and so purposeful that we feel an amazing sense of belonging and positivity as we move through the world.

This place of being is not something that is reserved for a select few. This place of being is accessible to *anyone and everyone.*

And the good news is, this place of being is not even hard to achieve. All you need to do is open your mind to the possibility that there is another way to live your life, and that there is a way to live a life that is filled with positive energy and magical opportunities. With this shift in awareness, with this openness to explore and start working with the energy of the Universe, you can start living a life that is bigger and more abundant than you could have ever imagined for yourself. You can start living a life that feels like it was designed specifically for you.

Any decision to change your life comes from a deep feeling of wanting something different for yourself, and from having an innate knowing that there is something better out there for you. This desire to change your life often creeps in when you start to awaken to the idea that all or part of your life is no longer fulfilling you and no longer serving you. For some people this feeling may show up as simply wanting a life that is free from the clutches of fear and anxiety. For others, this feeling may show up as wanting a life that feels more purposeful and directed. Often this idea of change first comes as a whisper, but over time the feeling grows and grows until it demands you to take action. Those of us who take action are the ones who begin the journey of discovering the deeper meaning of life. It is this journey that then gives rise to the understanding of your energy, your purpose, and what your soul has come here to achieve.

If you want to shift your life in this direction, if you want to start aligning yourself with these forces, then you must start by claiming your power back. You have to be ready and willing to stand up and take responsibility for your life and own every thought, experience, and feeling as if you chose it. When you regain this level of power, you can take the steps you need to shift your life in a positive direction.

WHO ARE YOU?

You are an amazing, complex, Divine being who is essentially composed of a soul, a mind, and a body. As you begin to understand the nature of who you are, it may allow you a glimpse into your potential and why you are here on this earthly journey. But who are you on the deepest level?

Are you the voices in your head? While hundreds of thoughts race through your mind, you are not those thoughts and you are not those voices. You are the *observer* of those thoughts; you are the one listening to them. As the observer of your thoughts, you have control over which thoughts you choose to believe and which thoughts you choose to ignore. At any given moment you have power to change the thoughts flowing in and the thoughts flowing out.

Even though you are not your thoughts, it is the thoughts that you hold on to or give the most attention to that shape how you view your life and the world around you.

So, if you are not your thoughts or the voices in your head even as you observe them, are you therefore your physical body? While in this physical realm, you are bound to your physical body, but what makes your physical body come alive? Simply, it is your life force energy—the energy of your soul—that is the true energy of who you are. Even though your physical body has a pulse, it is your soul that animates your body and brings life to it.

You are not your body and you are not your mind; *you are soul energy.* You are soul energy merely inhabiting a body for a brief period of time. This body and this mind is just a temporary home that your soul energy has chosen to operate from so that it may fulfill a higher purpose.

At your very core, you are a soul that was given a body and a mind. Your body and mind are temporary tools to help you on your journey. But often these tools can dominate your life, making you forget that you are more than just what you see. To live a positively charged life, you have to learn how to balance your mind, body, and soul, and allow them to operate as one. In order to do this, you need to allow your soul to be the guiding force. Your soul is the core of who you are and everything that emanates from your soul is helping you live a positive life. If you imagine you are a flower, then your soul is the seed. If you plant the seed, nourish and water it, and give it adequate sunlight, the rest takes care of itself. When you can tune in to the power of your soul, your mind and body will naturally follow.

WHY ARE YOU HERE?

You are here because you asked to be here. When you found out you were coming into this life with this body, this family, and this set of circumstances, your soul rejoiced, your soul was bursting with excitement, and your soul was thrilled at the possibility of coming through as You. Your soul came into your body for one very specific reason, and that is to grow. Growth is what keeps the Universe alive. Without the expansion of growth and consciousness, the Universe would wither away and there would be no creative fuel to manifest life.

So, even if it may not always feel like it, you are here because you wanted to be here. You are here because your soul wanted to enter and bring life to your body so it could grow, learn, fulfill your purpose, and experience the world in the third dimension. When your soul entered your body, it knew and understood that you may forget that it is there. It knew and understood that you may start identifying with your physical body or the physical world that you live in. It knew that you would want to experience the passion and emotions of life.

Your soul knew that you might forget about it; so at times, your soul may remind you of its presence. These reminders may come as whispers or a loud bang. It's even possible that these reminders may come in the form of a book, like the one you are holding in your hand.

YOUR SOUL ON EARTH

If you want to know what your ultimate purpose for being here is, then you need to rediscover your soul. Your soul is at the core of who you really are. When your soul came to earth, it came equipped with everything that it needed to fulfill your purpose and your destiny.

Your soul carries lifetimes of intelligence and is full of intuitive wisdom. When you learn to tap into your soul and connect with it, all the answers you have ever searched for will always be available to you, and you will be able to see your life unfolding from a new state of awareness.

The first step to connecting to your soul is understanding the nature of your soul and how it operates. Your soul is made of pure energy. This energy is the same energy that makes up everything in the entire Universe. You are simply the Universe expressing itself as a human. Reflect on that for just a moment—you are the Universe existing in a human shell. Inside of you is the entire Universe. This means that you are not *in* the Universe, you are actually the Universe yourself with a living and breathing pulse. This means that you are ultimately connected to everything around you. This concept can be difficult to wrap your head around at first, but when you start to sit with this thought, you begin to awaken to the infinite, magical potential that exists within you.

THE ENERGY OF YOUR SOUL

Your soul's energy is very similar to the energy or feeling of unconditional love. This love is bigger than most of us on earth can fathom with our rational minds. This love is so pure and so unconditional that when you do experience it, you feel so supported and so comforted that there is nothing in life you feel like you can't achieve. We all came from this love and we will all return to this love, and this powerful, loving energy lives inside all of us.

Your soul is endless and limitless. Because your soul is pure energy, it can never be destroyed; it simply shifts from one form to another. When your physical body dies, your soul continues to live on. Once your soul detaches from your physical body, your soul energy is so big and so large that it would be impossible to measure. It is timeless, boundless, and infinite. There is nothing your soul cannot do and there is nothing your soul cannot achieve.

Feel Your Soul Energy Right Now!

If you want to feel your soul energy right now, here is a quick trick: Rub your hands together until you feel a charge between them, and then very slowly pull your hands apart. Do you feel the heat and buzzing energy radiating between your two hands? That is your soul energy. The stronger your soul energy becomes, the more it is going to be able to guide and shape your life. As you read this book and start to adopt certain changes in your life, notice how this energetic charge strengthens.

All of us have the power and potential to explore the realm of infinite possibilities that our soul provides. We all have the ability to tap into the energy of our soul and be active participants in the creation of the Universe. We have the ability to co-create our reality and our destiny by awakening to the energy of our soul. When you understand this, it allows you to feel one with life. It allows you to feel that life is not happening to you, but rather life is happening *for* you.

Exercise: Ten-Minute Soul Connection Meditation

Meditation is an excellent tool for connecting with the energy of your soul and tapping into the essence of who you truly are. Even if you have never meditated before, give this simple exercise a try. The more frequently you practice it, the easier it will become and the more likely you are to experience the power and connection that comes from realigning with your soul.

1. Sit or lay down in a comfortable position and close your eyes. Still your mind by breathing in and out deeply at least five or six times.
2. If any thoughts come up, don't resist them; simply allow them to pass without engaging in them. Imagine your thoughts as leaves floating down a stream—they are there, but you are just looking at them, observing them as they go by.
3. Now take your awareness to your heart and imagine a radiant white light beaming gently from inside your heart. Keep your focus on your heart for a moment and try to feel the warm glow of this light.
4. Slowly imagine this light getting bigger and bigger as it starts to take up more space in your body. Visualize the light getting bigger and stronger and more vibrant until it has covered your entire body and is shooting out around you.
5. Bathe in this light and feel how nourishing, protective, and magical it is. Allow yourself to continue to release this white light from the strength of your heart.

6. Perhaps now you may begin to feel tingles or the gentle hum of your soul.
7. Finish the meditation by gently coming back into the awareness of your physical body and opening your eyes.

THE AWAKENING PROCESS

Awakening is the process of becoming aware of your energy, of the energy around you, and how to use this energy to create a life that feels fulfilling and connected. It is the process of discovering why you are here, who you really are, and your infinite potential. Awakening is simply about coming into a new level of awareness, and part of this new awareness is understanding that you are more than just your body and more than just your mind.

Think of awakening like the most powerful ah-ha moment of your life—a knowledge that shakes you so deeply that your entire life starts to shift and change. After viewing yourself as just a three-dimensional being, awakening allows you to understand that you are so much more than what you can see, almost as if you have opened your eyes to the fullness and energy of what surrounds you for the very first time.

Your awakening process may be particular to you, but you will begin it like everyone else: with a strong, burning desire to take control of your life and change its direction; to take responsibility for your life and the energy that you put out into the Universe. It starts with a fierce longing to stop seeing life in just one color and instead experience every color of the rainbow. Suddenly there is a force that feels bigger and brighter than you. Suddenly there is a force so grand and so strong that when it moves through your body, your entire being can't help but feel electrified. This impulse causes you to open your eyes and see life in a new way. This impulse stems from your desire to change, and helps you to start the awakening process.

Awakening is magical and beautiful, but it can also be painful because it requires you to come face to face with all the fears and past hurts that you may have buried away, denied, or ignored. In order to awaken to who you are, you have to peel back all the layers that you have collected over the years and start seeing yourself as you truly are. These layers are essentially conscious or unconscious blocks or barriers that you have built up around yourself out of fear, self-doubt, pain, or lack of confidence. Often these layers are formed out of protection, but over time they can create blockages that can inhibit you from moving forward and leave you feeling stuck. When you peel back these layers, you can start to awaken to the true potential of your life. When you've returned to your soul energy, you can love yourself and start expressing yourself from a true, authentic place. When you can just be unapologetically you, when you can tap into that inner essence and understand your power and divinity—that is when you will feel at one with life. That is when you will awaken.

To create this level of shift in your life, you have to be ready and willing to stand up and take responsibility for your every thought, experience, and feeling. You have to be willing to take ownership over your life, face your fears, and understand that your happiness is only yours to control. It is when you find this level of power in your life that you can take the steps to shift your life in a positive direction.

HOW AWAKENINGS CAN UNFOLD

The good news is that you don't have to have your entire journey figured out before you begin. You just have to be willing to commit to starting. When you do start, it is almost like the path will unfold as if by magic. In fact, most awakening processes happen organically and in a natural way. Even though awakenings don't always happen in stages, they do usually follow a pattern. This pattern, outlined in the list that follows, is not designed for you to emulate; rather, it is provided to help you understand the flow of the awakening journey:

1. You are unhappy or confused about the current state of your life. You want to change because your old ways of operating don't seem to be working for you. You feel unsupported by life and the opportunities that have been presented to you. This frustration and pain builds and builds. Your uneasy and unsatisfied feelings become so overwhelming that you no longer can tolerate living your life the way you currently are. From this place of darkness, frustration, and questioning, you begin to understand that your life doesn't *have* to be this way and that there is an alternative. Your awareness begins to expand, and when you really look at yourself and who you are, a part of you that has been asleep for a very long time begins to awaken.
2. With eyes open, you start to view your life in a different way. The fog around your life has been lifted and suddenly you realize how your actions, thoughts, and behaviors have created the reality that you now sit in. During this phase, you start questioning some of the decisions you have made, which in turn causes

you to feel confronted with a host of emotions. Fears from your past and present begin to rise up, and fears of your future begin to crop up. You start to question everything, and you start to challenge what you previously knew to be true.

3. You feel overwhelmed and you wonder if it is better to just go back to "sleep." Your beliefs, thoughts, and patterns are all shifting and you start to ponder deep questions: What is my purpose? Why am I here? Why have I been tolerating the life I have been living? You again realize that you can no longer operate your life in the same way that you had been doing, but this awareness causes a rush of fear. Now you are faced with a decision to make: Do you go back to sleep or do you continue to awaken? For those who continue to awaken, a transformation begins to occur.

4. These deeper questions and bubbling emotions start to cause internal shifts, which then give rise to external shifts. Once you start seeing things in this new way, you can no longer hide your truth. Certain negative things around you begin melting away—friends who never had your best interests, your job that you don't feel passionate about, your relationship that never felt fulfilling. All the things that no longer serve you, all the things that you were holding on to out of fear, begin to slip away. The beauty of this stage is that it allows you to confront your fears face to face, so you can transcend them.

5. As the things that no longer serve you begin to drop away, you begin feeling excited and inspired by what is next. People may tell you that you have changed, or that there is some-

thing different about you. You begin to seek answers to life's deeper questions, you seek out relevant reading material, and your interest in spirituality starts to grow. You begin intuitively understanding that you are a powerful and magical being who has the ability to create and manifest things. You start to realize the interconnectedness of all things; you start to realize that you are a part of the Universe.

6. By aligning with your true, authentic self, you realize that your only purpose in this life is to be true to who you are and that everything about your life is perfect and just as it should be. At this stage of your awakening, there are no limits as to where you can go.

When you become aware that you are more than just your body and your thoughts, it starts a deeper questioning process that forces you to really assess how you have been living your life. With fresh eyes and a new perspective, perhaps you start to realize that you are not living a life that makes you truly feel alive; perhaps you realize that there are some changes to make; perhaps you realize that all along, the only person that was holding you back was you.

MY OWN AWAKENING

I know this process intimately because I have been through it myself. Many years ago, I was miserable with my life. I felt useless and worthless. I felt like I didn't belong, that life had no use for me. I was gripped with feelings of low self-esteem and low self-worth and felt that the world was a harsh place that was out to get me. I felt powerless to change my reality and would instead wallow in my misery. As you can imagine, this was not a fun way to live life. Life had no meaning; life had no magic. It was dull and boring and every day trickled by painfully.

The pain grew and grew until it was so large that it encompassed every aspect of who I was. This caused me to hate myself, hate my life, and hate my body. Every flaw was amplified, every painful emotion was strengthened, and every feeling of hopelessness was highlighted. Eventually, I became physically sick and this further fueled my feelings of self-hatred and loathing. For years, I struggled to accept who I was and the life that was unfolding around me. I felt that life had served me a great disservice by giving me a family who didn't understand me, friends who didn't support me, and a body that was failing me. It wasn't until I felt so abandoned by everything and everyone that I realized if I wanted a change, it was going to have to come from me. If I wanted to shift things, I was going to have to start with myself. This finally allowed me to take the power of my life into my own hands. This finally allowed me to step up and out of my misery and into a place of action. Finally, I stepped up and said, "Enough! I can't tolerate this anymore. I don't want to live like this anymore, I want something better for myself." When I did this, my entire life changed.

"And then one day, I discovered my own light, my own inner-gangster. I snatched my power back and the game changed."

—Unknown

The change happened on an internal level first and then seeped out into my entire life. I started reading inspirational books, surrounded myself with positive energy, and tried to look at things from a more positive perspective. Suddenly, I started feeling drawn to things that made me feel good. Then I became drawn to things I felt passionate about, and my entire life started to change and shift into a more positive place. My friends and family around me noticed too, and they commented on how happy and vibrant I looked. Even though I was the same person, I felt reborn, almost like a part of me that I had carried around for so long had died and had been rebirthed into something new. I felt awakened and I felt alive. I felt as if there was nothing I couldn't achieve, do, or be, and this drive is what propelled me into finding myself, finding my calling, and writing this book.

Exercise: Understanding Your Own Awakening Process

Just the fact that you have even taken an interest in this book shows that you have already begun to awaken on some level. Everyone's awakening process will manifest differently and will vary in intensity. It is also possible that your awakening process will go back and forth across different stages, depending where you are in your life and your level of awareness.

In this exercise, you will reflect on the different awakenings you have already experienced in your life, whether they were small ah-ha moments or bigger life-changing moments:

1. Reflect on three "ah-ha" awakening moments in your life that allowed you to step up and make a powerful change. How did these moments change the direction of your life?
2. How can you use the realizations that your past awakening(s) offered to you in your life today? How can you use these realizations to help you claim your power back right now?

Sometimes all it takes to change your life to this level is claiming your own power back. No one else is responsible for you, your happiness, and your feelings of joy, except you. So, if you are ready to reclaim your power, if you are ready to make positive changes in your life, then know it all begins with saying "Enough!" And then trusting what unfolds next.

AWAKENING TO YOUR SOUL ENERGY

When you start awakening to the realization that you are so much more than just your mind and your body, the frequency of your energy begins to rise and expand. You may even feel the force of the soul energy that lives inside of you radiating out of your being. In fact, the stronger you can connect with your soul energy, the higher your consciousness or awareness is going to expand.

While it may be difficult to feel your soul energy at first, it is likely that you have already felt it numerous times throughout your life without actually realizing it. Your soul energy is most strong when you are doing things that you love to do. For example, think back to a time when you:

- Did something that made you feel calm and joyous.
- Felt so passionately about something or so overcome with positive emotions that tears started to well in the corner of your eyes.
- Laughed so hard that you almost couldn't breathe.

These responses are examples of your soul energy. The more you strengthen this force, the more often you will feel these amazing emotional responses.

CHAPTER WRAP-UP

You have felt that inner spark, that inner fire rising up and out of your soul and into your consciousness. That inner magic confirms that you are a vibrant, creative, full being who is here to experience joy. You have been awakened to this feeling and perhaps you picked up this book, wondering if you can get more of that feeling. You absolutely can, and it all starts with reclaiming your power.

When you can step into that inner spark, that inner magic, that inner fire, and claim it—that is when you will awaken. That is when you will come face to face with the power of who you truly are.

- You are more than just a body and you are more than just a mind, you are soul energy.
- Your mind and body are temporary things that were given to you to help fulfill the purpose and mission of your soul.
- You are here in this life and in this body because your soul asked to be here.
- By understanding that you are soul energy, it allows you to awaken and tap into your true potential and power.
- When you reclaim your power and take responsibility for your life, you can start to make positive changes that feel aligned with your soul.
- When you connect with your soul, you naturally align with the life that was meant for you, which is the most positive life you can achieve.

CHAPTER 2

THE POWER OF ENERGY

You are pure, potential energy and whatever tune your energy has, whatever melody it makes, determines your purpose on this earth and in the Universe.

ENERGY BASICS

Everything in the Universe vibrates at a particular frequency, including you.

We are all energetic beings that live in an energetic Universe. When you break everything down to the deepest molecular level, we are all made of the same ingredients; we are all just atoms. These atoms contain energy that vibrates at a particular frequency. These collective vibrations create an energy field that connects you with everything in the Universe.

Energy, Around the World

Many ancient and sacred texts have acknowledged the existence of this energy field. In China they refer to it as "Chi"; in India it is referred to as "Prana"; in ancient Egypt they called it "Ka"; and in the West it is referred to as the "life force" or "universal life force." No matter what you call it, this energetic charge forms the foundation of everything in our Universe and links us all together as one and the same.

It is not necessary to fully understand or comprehend this concept in order to work with it. In fact, the very nature of the Universe may make it truly impossible to completely understand. But by simply opening to the idea that you are energy existing in an energetic Universe, you can begin to understand your infinite potential.

LIVING IN AN ENERGETIC UNIVERSE

Even though at your core you are soul energy, you also have a mind and a body that cannot be ignored. In an energetic Universe, it is not just your soul that has energy: Every thought you have, every action you take, and every feeling that is emitted from your being carries energy. This energy is beamed out into the Universe and creates part of the reality that you live, see, and experience.

What Is Positive Energy?

Positive energy is anything that makes you feel good, and feeling good happens when a vibration resonates with your soul.

You may have heard the phrase "looking through life with rose-colored glasses," but in truth we are all viewing reality through the lens of our own mind. Because we live in an energetic Universe, everything around us is responding to our energy and vice versa. Almost like the world around us is one giant mirror reflecting back our energetic state. To visualize this, let's use colors to paint a picture.

In an energetic Universe, like attracts like, which means that whatever energy you are emanating from your entire being is simply going to attract more of that energy back to you. If you start thinking blue thoughts, you are going to attract blue thoughts. If you start thinking yellow thoughts, you are going to start attracting yellow thoughts. Let's say that over the years, the energy of your entire being turns yellow. This means that every thought, every action, and every word that comes from you is also tinted yellow. Thus the entire world in which you see, live, and operate is yellow. You could even say that you are viewing life through "yellow-tinted glasses." When living in a yellow world it can be very difficult for you to see other colors, and it can be very difficult for you to comprehend things outside of your yellow world. To you, everything is just yellow.

In many ways, the energetic Universe operates in the same way. If you are always thinking the same thoughts, you are always going to keep getting more of the same experiences that confirm those thoughts. In other words, what you think, feel, and focus on you attract and receive into your life. If you focus on blue, you get blue. If you focus on yellow, you get yellow. Whatever energy you are emitting, whatever color you are attracting into your life, paints your experiences and shapes the life that you lead.

Once you understand this, you may start to become aware that everything you are experiencing and seeing in your life is limited by the colored lens you are seeing it through. We all have a lens through which we see and experience the world, and no lens color is better or worse than the other. The aim here instead is to align the color of your lens with what you want to attract; and what you want to attract are experiences that are aligned with your mind, body, and soul. When you sync up your mind, body, and soul to operate on the same energetic frequency, then true magic can occur.

YOUR ENERGETIC FREQUENCY FINDS MORE ENERGY LIKE IT

Now that you are starting to understand that your energetic state or frequency determines what you see and what you focus on, you can begin to understand how to create a more positive life. To give you an example, if you are constantly thinking about how badly someone has treated you and how they wronged you, chances are your feelings of being mistreated or being wronged are only going to amplify. This in turn makes you more and more upset and causes you to focus on all the bad things that this person has done to you. Conversely, the more positively focused your mind is, the more likely you are to notice the positive experiences in any given situation and the more likely you are to see every experience as an opportunity to learn and grow.

> *"Loving people live in a loving world. Hostile people live in a hostile world. Same world."*
>
> —Wayne Dyer

Everything about you—from your upbringing to your environment to the thoughts that run through your head—creates the life that you lead. It doesn't necessarily mean that your thoughts control your reality; instead, your thoughts *shape* how you view your reality. We all live in the same world, but our experiences of it will be different, depending on our energy and our vibration.

WHAT IS AN ENERGETIC VIBRATION?

We are all made of energy, and all energy vibrates at a particular frequency. This frequency is determined by the thoughts and feelings we emit. Certain feelings, such as fear, anger, guilt, self-loathing, and lack of self-worth, vibrate at a low frequency, meaning that the energy moves slower. Energies like love, joy, laughter, abundance, gratitude, healing, miracles, and a sense of purpose vibrate at a higher frequency, meaning that the energy moves faster.

Everyone's vibrations are continually being sent out into the Universe. These vibrations allow the Universe to create. It is almost like the Universe takes all these collective vibrations and morphs them into the physical reality that we all see and experience.

We all live in the same world, but your energetic vibration dictates how you see the world. People who are vibrating on a higher frequency tend to be able to see the positive side to any situation, whereas people operating on a lower frequency tend to only be able to focus on the negatives. When you operate from a higher vibration, you attract or notice higher vibrational things. When you operate from a lower vibration, you may attract or notice lower vibrational things. You may have experienced this effect in your life: When you start off your day in a bad mood, things just seem to get progressively worse and worse, unless you can snap out of it and shift your mindset.

LOWER VIBRATIONAL ENERGY

Have you ever met someone who just gives you bad vibes for no particular reason? If you have ever met anyone who seems to give off negative energy or has low energy, it is likely they are operating on a low vibration. We all move up and down the frequency levels of our vibration. While being in a low vibration frequency is okay at times, you definitely don't want to live here all the time. When you are feeling sad or drained, your vibration is often dimmed. When you operate from a lower vibration over time, you tend to attract lower vibrational people and experiences into your life. These can lead you to feeling miserable and stuck, and can also make it harder for you to feel good or positive about your life.

Things that lower your vibration include:

- Complaining
- Toxic relationships
- Holding on to the past
- Holding on to fears
- An inability to forgive
- Self-hatred or putting yourself down
- Resentment or jealousy
- Guilt
- Eating processed foods
- Exposure to pollution or toxic chemicals found in household cleaning supplies, cosmetics, and the like

Essentially, anything that makes you feel miserable or aims to cover up or hide your true thoughts and feelings can lower your vibration and cause you to attract experiences that are not aligned with your soul energy.

HOW TO MOVE OUT OF LOW VIBRATIONS

Beating yourself up for partaking in lower vibrational experiences can lower your vibration further, so forget the blame and the guilt. Instead, just start shifting your mindset to something more positive and loving in order to help you raise the frequency of your vibrations. Throughout the coming weeks, pay attention to any negative thoughts that occur and see if you can switch your thinking to something more positive. Maybe you can find a new way to look at the situation that allows you to focus on gratitude. The more you practice this, the better at it you will become and the easier it will be for you to keep your vibration humming at the perfect level for you.

Not All Negative Thoughts Are Bad

It is important to also remember that not all negative thoughts are necessarily bad. Darker emotions are powerful teachers that can help you put things into perspective. Think of it this way: If we never felt anger, then we would never know what it was like to truly be calm and peaceful; if we never felt sadness, we wouldn't know what it is like to experience true happiness. Because emotions like anger are so strong they often lead us to our truth more quickly than some of the softer or gentler emotions. For this reason, there is no need to shy away from heavy emotions; instead it is important to stand up and pay attention whenever they arise. These heavy emotions only contribute to a lowered vibration when they are left to fester or are not processed and released.

Often, our heavy emotions like anger stick around because we fear seeing the truth or accepting things as they are. In fact, the emotions that we hold on to are often the emotions we have not dealt with. So, if you feel negative emotions bubbling to the surface, allow them in. By doing this, you will be able to sit with them, learn from them, and release them. Engaging in this process is far more powerful than hiding your negative emotions or smothering them with fake positive thinking.

Positive thinking really only works when it comes from a genuine place, so don't trick or force yourself into thinking positive thoughts because it is the "right" thing to do. The right thing to do is to express your truth of how you really feel at your core. Usually, when your true feelings are expressed, they evaporate. But if you find that you are expressing yourself and still feeling the same way, it may be that you need to dig a little deeper and get to the root of what your true feelings are. Often emotions like anger are surface-level emotions that hide things like pain or sadness. So, if lashing out and expressing your anger is not serving you, it could be that you need to venture a little deeper to uncover the truth of what you are really feeling.

Exercise: Release with the Breath

Breathing can be a powerful way to release heavy emotions quickly. Start by taking three to five deep breaths in and out. Then on your next inhale, imagine breathing in calming white light. As you breathe this in, visualize the white light soothing and calming your mind, body, and spirit. Then as you exhale, visualize the heavy emotions leaving your body as clouds of smoke. Repeat this a few times until you feel calm, centered, and at peace.

HOW TO RELEASE NEGATIVE ENERGY

You can try to run away from negative emotions like frustration, anger, fear, or pain, but the truth is you can't. You can try to avoid or suppress them, but try as you might, they will remain and start to take over your life. Until you can actually face your pain, until you can actually face your fears head on, they will run your life. To confront your fears and pain, you don't need to have it all figured out. You simply have to sit with them and give yourself permission to really allow yourself to feel them. Sometimes the single most healing thing you can do for yourself is allow yourself to feel.

This feeling process is the easiest way to move through negative emotions. This process helps you to understand where the negative emotions are coming from and what they are trying to show you. Allowing an emotion in and really feeling it can be challenging, but it allows you to actually process the feeling. Once the emotion is felt and processed, it no longer needs to linger. When you resist an emotion, it will persist. But when you allow it in, it will show you what it needs to show you, and then it will fizzle out.

HIGHER VIBRATIONAL ENERGY

On the flip side of negative energy, if you are positive and in a good mood, your vibration is often supercharged. When your energy vibrates at a higher frequency, it allows you to attract more *positive* experiences into your life. It is not that the world around you will change into some mythical utopia, but your perception of the world and how you see and deal with things will change. Some examples include:

- Solutions will present themselves; you will feel less stressed and less anxious.
- You will be able to make decisions based not in fear, but in love.
- You will feel supported to go after your dreams and inspired by the world around you.
- You will feel safe and comforted and provided for.

When you shift your mindset in this direction, life takes on a whole new meaning and problems aren't as daunting. You'll still face problems, of course, but you will have the strength to handle them in the best way possible.

HOW TO RAISE YOUR VIBRATION

When you feel good, your energy or vibration begins to rise. The highest frequency in the Universe is unconditional love, followed by other feel-good emotions, including gratitude, enthusiasm, compassion, joy, and peace. To raise your energetic vibration, therefore, you want to seek out anything that makes you feel these uplifting emotions. For example:

- **Breathe deeply:** Breathing instantly calms your mind and body, and it allows you to access peace and serenity. The best part? You can do it anywhere, anytime.
- **Laugh out loud:** We all know how good it feels to laugh. It's no wonder—laughing can quickly raise your vibration. Find a funny video clip online to get yourself laughing.
- **Smile:** Similar to laughing, smiling can also raise your vibration and allow you to feel an instant sense of joy. If you're having trouble finding something to smile about, think of a pleasant memory or look at a photo of your favorite person.
- **Be grateful:** Expressing appreciation for the things or people in your life is another way to boost your vibration. You can think small (feeling thankful for your morning cup of coffee) or big (being grateful for your powerful and all-loving soul)!

- **Eat raw food:** Raw, organically grown foods contain their own vital energy, and by eating these foods frequently, you can help boost your vibration. Look for in-season, local options at farmers' markets.
- **Exercise:** Moving your body helps to increase the flow of energy and releases "feel-good" brain chemicals, which also helps boost your vibration. Whether it's a sport you've been playing for years or a brand-new hobby, get your body moving and start enjoying the physical and spiritual benefits of exercise.
- **Get out in nature:** Spending time outside is a natural way to heal body and mind. It can also boost your energy levels and vibration, and will help you feel calm and peaceful. If you're in a city or busy area, find a green oasis in a park or courtyard.
- **Meditate:** Meditation calms your mind and expands your consciousness, which naturally helps lift your vibration. You'll find several meditation exercises in this book to use as a starting point.
- **Use positive thinking:** As we'll discuss throughout this book, focusing on positive thoughts is one of the best ways to raise your energy levels and vibration.

Essentially, anything that makes you feel good will help you raise your vibration. So the more you can focus on feeling good, the stronger and more powerful your vibration is going to become.

CARING FOR YOUR ENERGY

While creating positive energy starts on the inside, your external environment plays a vital role in the type of energy you create in your life. In order to create positive energy at every level, you have to be mindful about who you surround yourself with, what you surround yourself with, and what foods you choose to put into your body.

Living in a densely populated city illustrates the challenges of balancing inner energy with external forces. In such a city, it is very easy to get overwhelmed or even distracted by the sheer amount of energy around you. No matter how positive or supercharged your energy may be, living in a dense environment with lots of energy can take its toll on your overall vibration.

The same goes for your home or work environment. If you work in a very hostile or negative environment, it can be even more challenging to keep your spirits high and your vibration lifted. It can also be difficult to do this when you are surrounded with people who are unsupportive of you or who want to keep you stuck and miserable alongside them.

In most cases, when you start raising the vibration of your inside energy, the outside tends to take care of itself shortly thereafter. In the meantime, you may have to develop some tools of protection that can help to support and nourish your energy.

DO YOU NEED AN ENERGY CLEANSE?

Here are some common signs that your energy is in need of cleansing:

- You have repetitive thoughts that constantly circle around in your mind.
- You feel guilty or regretful for decisions you have made in the past.

- You feel confused, stuck, or unmotivated in your life.
- You have a hard time accepting things and wish things were different than what they were.
- You feel wronged or taken advantage of by other people.
- You feel out of alignment with what is happening in your life.
- You feel drained and exhausted.
- You find yourself taking on other people's emotions.

TOOLS FOR PROTECTING YOUR ENERGY

Just like it is important to exercise and eat unprocessed foods in order to feel energized and cleansed on a physical level, you also need to pay attention and care for your energetic body as well. This means that you need to cleanse, protect, and nourish your energy in order to continue radiating positivity.

You can also think of this as your spiritual or energetic hygiene. This spiritual self-care is just as important as washing your hands, especially if you are surrounded by a toxic or negative environment. Because we are energetic beings, we have the ability to absorb and take on the energies of those around us. The same way we can transfer germs, we can also transfer energy.

Here are some tools that you can use to protect your energy:

- **Crystals:** Because of their pure energy and geometric structure, crystals have the ability to retain and transfer positive energy. This transfer of positive energy can help cleanse away any negative or stagnant energy. Crystals that are particularly good for protecting and cleansing your energy include clear quartz, smoky quartz, amethyst, fluorite, and black tourmaline.

- **White light:** Imagine yourself surrounded in a white light. This is a great way to protect your energy and clear away any negative energy that may be lingering in the air. To do this, simply visualize a powerful white light surrounding your entire body. Continue visualizing this in your mind's eye until you can clearly see the white light surrounding you and protecting you.
- **Smudging with sage or incense:** The smoke from sage or incense has been used for centuries to help clear the air and drive away negative energy. To do this, simply wave the smoke around the outline of your entire body and then your surroundings with the intention of cleansing and purifying. While you do this, make sure that you have a window open or proper ventilation so the smoke can carry the negative energy outside.
- **Sound healing:** Sound can be extremely healing and can also help you harmonize and realign your body. There are many different singing bowls that can help to balance the energy centers of the body. To pick the perfect one, simply listen to the sound and choose the one that resonates with you the most. Playing relaxing music or using a tuning fork in the frequency of love, 528 Hz, can also help to clear negative energy from your space and body.
- **Essential oils:** Essential oils carry nature's innate healing vibration at a very high potency. Essential oils that are great for energy clearing include sandalwood, rose, white sage, frankincense, and patchouli. Simply take the oil and dab a small amount behind your neck. If you have sensitive skin, you may want to mix the essential oil in a moisturizer or carrier oil.

Exercise: A Positive Energy Cleanse

A positive energy cleanse can help to kick-start a powerful change. Here's how to do it:

1. Find a quiet place where you can't be disturbed and then begin writing all your thoughts, feelings, and emotions on a piece of paper. Don't hold back; keep writing until all the thoughts that are swimming around in your mind are out on the paper. You may have to challenge yourself to keep writing even if your ideas are not flowing, as this will help to build momentum. Aim to write for at least three to four pages, back and front.
2. Once you have all your deepest thoughts and feelings out on paper, take a moment to allow yourself to feel all the emotions that are arising. Then take your pieces of paper and begin ripping them up as a sign of letting go. With each rip, keep affirming that you are ready to let go of the past and any negative energy so that you can welcome in the positive.
3. Place your hands on your belly and begin breathing in and out. Practice breathing deep into your belly so you are filling your entire body with oxygen. As you breathe in, feel your rib cage and belly expand; and as you exhale, feel your rib cage and belly contract. Once you have taken a few deep breaths, close your eyes and on every inhale imagine that you are breathing in a cleansing, positive white light; and on every exhale, imagine

you are releasing all the negative energy in clouds of black smoke. As you inhale, visualize your entire body filling with this amazing positive energy; and as you exhale, really push out all the dark clouds that have been attached to you for so long. Repeat this process for at least ten breaths.

4. Now, take a fresh sheet of paper and begin writing what you would like to fill your life with. Begin writing about all the positive blessings that you would like to attract and all the positive blessings that are currently in your life. Write down whatever comes to your mind, just try to keep your words positive and loving.
5. Once you have written your positive blessings, fold up the piece of paper and place it over your heart. Repeat this affirmation (or you can even write your own): *"I cleanse my mind, body, and soul so I may receive the blessings of every moment as they arise. I cleanse my mind, body, and soul so I may feel gratitude and ease every single day. Through this cleanse, I fill my life with positive energy and guidance from the Divine spark that lives within me and all around me. As I surround myself in positive energy, my life becomes a blessing and joy, and I feel restored and deeply at peace."*

Recite this affirmation daily to help continue with the cleansing process and to keep inviting positive energy into your life.

UNCONDITIONAL LOVE: THE MOST POWERFUL ENERGY IN THE UNIVERSE

When you lead your life in connection with your soul, you move through the world attuned to a higher vibrational frequency. This is because your soul vibrates on the same frequency as unconditional love. Unconditional love is the most powerful and positive force in the Universe. When you operate from the place of unconditional love, your ability to manifest and create things in your physical reality becomes supercharged, almost as if you were given magical powers.

It is not necessary for you to do anything in order to achieve feelings of unconditional love because essentially that is what you are made of already. What you have to put effort into, however, is remembering that you came from this place.

If we are all unconditional love and we will all return to unconditional love, this means every experience and every circumstance that we find ourselves in is ultimately for our highest good and the highest good of the Universe. Even though it may not seem that way when you are going through a difficult circumstance, every experience that comes your way is a powerful lesson and teacher. At the end of the day, if unconditional love flows through you and around you and essentially is you, you will always be supported and always be loved, no matter what.

LIVING FROM A PLACE OF UNCONDITIONAL LOVE

Unconditional love is all very well and good, but how do you actually apply it to your everyday life? Is it really possible to love everyone unconditionally?

Whether you realize it or not, you are unconditionally loving everyone to the best of your abilities at all times. It may not always feel that way, but because that is who you are at your core, it has to also be part of what you offer to others.

Many people think that unconditional love means allowing someone to walk all over you and loving them anyway, but that is not really what it is about. *Unconditional love is about being true to who you are and living from a place of complete authenticity.* When you operate from a place of true and pure authenticity, you operate from your soul, and the only thing you can offer from your soul is unconditional love.

"Unconditional love" may not be the best words to use to define this Universal love energy that we all are because of the associations many of us hold about love. Regardless, the concept of unconditional love can help us realize that we are all connected and that we are all the same. We are all tiny fragments of the Universe, which means that our energy is all made up of the same thing. Our energy is also connected precisely because we are all made up of the same thing. Of course, we all have different personalities, looks, and traits, but deep down on a core level, we are all made up of the same energy. Surrounding this energy, we have our own mind, our own emotions, and our own physical body. These components combined give us the sum of who we are. Through our minds and bodies, we develop our differences, and these differences allow us to bring our energy into the world in a unique way.

In fact, taking this unconditional love energy that is inside of us and mixing it with our different personality traits, skills, passions, and desires allows us to fulfill our life's purpose. By understanding who we are at our core, plus embracing all the unique traits that make us special, we can start to feel connected to our purpose and what we are here to achieve. Many times, however, people reject these unique traits and feel embarrassed or scared to express them. We instead stick to what everyone else is doing and ignore any inkling to stray from the tried-and-true path. We get caught up in fears and societal pressures to be or look a certain way, and we lose sight of our own colors and the unique spark that we came into this world with. Conformity is rooted in fear, and this fear of wanting to fit in causes a lot of people to simply start operating on autopilot. They move from one day to the next doing the same thing over and over again, never really questioning if what they are doing is fulfilling or if they are making good choices. Often living life this way is a sign of being trapped in fear and of exhibiting a lack of trust in yourself and the world around you, but there is a way forward. And by reading this book, you have already started to make tracks.

UNCONDITIONAL LOVE AND POSITIVE ENERGY

Unconditional love and positive energy work hand in hand. In fact, you can't truly be positive unless you first access the energy of unconditional love. A few years ago, I started working at a job that sounded amazing in the description but in reality was definitely not as advertised. My boss was also very aggressive and would often yell and belittle everyone who worked there, including me. I needed the money and was afraid of being without a job, so I continued to work there while looking for something else on the side. I had the financial security of my job, which made it very difficult for me to stay motivated to keep looking for something else.

Eventually, I gave up on leaving and decided to try my best to make peace with where I was. Every day, I dreaded going to work. Even though I tried to be positive and tried to look at things differently, I still felt miserable and upset on the inside. At this stage, I knew that my thoughts were powerful so I continued to visualize and practice positive thinking in order to get through the day. It worked, but in many ways it was a temporary fix. It helped me to get through the day, but inside I was still feeling like I was stuck in a job that I really didn't want. I continued to pressure myself to think positively, to try and focus on all the things that I enjoyed about the job.

About a year into the job, I had enough of feeling miserable and was tired of fighting to stay positive, so I decided to quit. I didn't have any backup plans. I just knew that I could not spend another day in that job because it was draining my energy and starting to make an impact on my overall well-being. On my last day, when I walked out of that place for good, I felt an incredible sense of joy and relief. I also felt clear about what my purpose had been at that job. The lesson was about learning to love myself. The lesson was about learning to say no. The lesson was about learning to not tolerate a place like that or put myself in a position like that ever again. In this situation, this was the most positive outcome I could give myself.

While the positive thinking definitely helped me endure my time at this workplace, I also needed to take positive *action* and love myself enough to remove myself from the situation. It was then I realized the real and true power of positive energy, and I allowed that positive energy to truly flow into my life.

Without unconditional love for yourself, any positive thinking will be stifled and will only be able to offer temporary relief. While positive thinking may be enough in some situations, it is only temporary unless you follow it up with a positive action—and the positive action can only come through loving yourself enough to take that meaningful step. If you truly want to shift your life to a positive frequency, you first have to start with unconditional self-love.

The Hidden Messages in Water

One book that changed my life forever was the *Hidden Messages in Water* by Dr. Masaru Emoto. Dr. Emoto reported in the 1990s that he believed water molecules were able to change shape based on the energy surrounding them. He would take water from different sources, freeze it, then place it under a microscope and examine the different shapes and patterns the water crystals would make. He wrote that the most beautiful crystals were from sources deep in nature where the land was untouched, whereas the water crystals from the tap and city lakes and streams were always misshapen and broken. Taking his studies further, he decided to say positive things to and give loving energy to the broken water crystals. Remarkably, when he did this, he said that the broken water crystals would change shape and begin healing. Over time, the broken and misshapen water crystals became perfectly formed and beautiful again. Because our own bodies are primarily made up of water, it is interesting to think of the possibility of this playing out in our own bodies in every single moment.

CHAPTER WRAP-UP

When you start to pay attention to the idea that you are an energetic being in an energetic Universe, suddenly you get access to a whole new way of living. Your energy is so powerful that you can use it to shift and change the way you perceive your world. By focusing on the things that make you feel good, you start to raise your vibration and shift into a state of positive energy. In this state, you attract more positive experiences and vibrations back to you.

- Everything in this Universe is vibrating, these vibrations create an energy field which we are all connected to.
- In this energetic Universe, like energy attracts like energy. Whatever energy you are emitting is going to be sent back to you.
- We are all experiencing reality through the lens of our own mind. By changing the lens of your mind to see things differently, you can change how you view your reality.
- Maintaining a positive frame of mind may not be possible 100 percent of the time, but if you operate from this place as much as possible, it will help to make your life much easier.
- In order to create a positive life, you need to raise your level of vibration. You do this through focusing on things that make you *feel* good.
- Your vibration can be lowered by negative emotions, thoughts, feelings, and even foods. When these negative vibrations linger for some time, they can change the way you view your reality and cause you to focus on only the negative things.
- Negative emotions are necessary for growth and development; they only affect your vibration when they are not cleared and released.

- Protecting and cleansing your energy is just as important as washing your hands and can help you to maintain a positive state of being and boost your energy levels.
- You are in charge of the energy you create through your thoughts, words, and attitude.

CHAPTER 3

THE MIRACULOUS ENERGY OF SELF-LOVE

If you want to see true magic, learn to really love yourself. When you do, everything else in your life will fall into place in the most miraculous of ways.

YOU ALREADY HAVE EVERYTHING YOU NEED

Some people believe that they have to be "perfect" in order to think positively and have a wonderful life. They fall into the trap of thinking that they need to look a certain way or have certain things, or prove something to themselves or others in order to be happy. But this is just not true.

You are already perfect; and you already have everything you need to start living a positive life. Just by being true to yourself, just by being authentic to your true nature, and just by believing in yourself, you can start to shift in a positive direction and change your life. There is nothing that you need to acquire and no magic recipe that you need to follow. Everything that you need is inside of you.

FOCUS ON YOU

Because everyone is unique, no one else's journey is going to look exactly the same as yours. We are all walking our own path, so be mindful not to compare your journey to the journey others are taking. At the end of the day, only you know what is best for you and only you know what feels right for you in your own heart. It doesn't matter if your decisions are not popular; it doesn't matter if your decisions may not be received well; what matters is that your decisions matter to you.

The best gift you can give yourself is to be true to who you are, and the only way you can start to do this is through learning to put yourself first. This is often viewed as being selfish. Many of us probably grew up believing that it is selfish to love ourselves. Indeed, society often advocates self-deprecation over self-respect. But putting yourself first is not an act of selfishness. Think of it this way: How can you expect to give and be of service to others when you are feeling drained or compromised? How genuine are your actions when you are acting from a place of guilt or expectation? In order to truly give to others and to the world, you have to put your own needs first and ensure that you are taken care of. Putting yourself first should be your top priority.

Balancing Caregiving and Self-Love

Of course, there often comes a time in life when you need to give and be of service to others before yourself. This is especially true if you have children or are responsible for caring for others. But if you find yourself continually compromising yourself even when caring for others, eventually you are going to find yourself burnt out and miserable. Living your life this way is not sustainable, no matter how much you love the person or people you are caring for. If you find yourself giving to the point where you feel depleted, the only way forward is to put your foot down and start taking responsibility for you. Determine what is the most compassionate and supportive thing that you can do for yourself, and then make it a priority to do it. It may be as simple as making yourself a cup of tea, or taking the time to relax in a hot bath, but get in the habit of asking yourself this question every single day. When you start to rejuvenate yourself and your energy through taking care of yourself, it is not only going to help you feel good, but it will also allow you to give back even more.

THE POWER OF SELF-OWNERSHIP

Making self-love a priority helps you create a more inspired and positive life, and it allows you to feel more comfortable and accepting of who you are. We all have things about our body that we wish we could change, and we all have areas of our lives that we wish to improve. But, if you chase the idea that you will only be happy once you achieve these changes in your life, you will never truly be happy. For true shift to occur, it has to happen within, which means that no amount of external shifts are going to work if you don't first address the internal shifts.

You have to learn how to love and accept yourself exactly as you are, flaws and all. It is only when you do this that you can really create lasting change in your life. Even if you lose those 20 pounds or buy the perfect house or win the lottery . . . if you are not happy from within, those changes won't affect your overall outlook. All the cosmetic fixes and all the money in the world can only buy you a temporary sliver of happiness. After that wears off, your attention will immediately turn to another flaw or issue. For true, lasting happiness, you need to learn to feel happy with exactly where you are and with exactly what you have. You have to accept and learn to love yourself and your life no matter what. When you do this, it becomes a lot easier to make lasting changes that are actually fulfilling. It also helps release any expectation or pressure that you may be putting on yourself and, more important, it also gives you your power back. By placing your happiness in a future event or in the hands of another person, it makes it very difficult for you to take ownership of your life and appreciate your own rhythm and melody.

LOVING YOURSELF

Inside all of us is a treasure chest of tools, inspirations, and ideas that we can use to live the life that was destined for us.

Our own fears and doubts, however, can close the lid on this treasure chest making us forget that we have access to all this information within our very own soul. We forget about our power and who we really are.

Our souls are so powerful and so infinite, they can create anything that we put our minds to, but so many of us reject our soul. We get caught up in thoughts like, "I am not good enough" or "I can't have this because I am dumb/poor/ugly." So many of us reject our inner power and our inner potential, and we forget that located within we have everything we need to live the life destined for us. We reject this "within" energy, we reject ourselves . . . and the treasure chest lies forgotten and buried in self-hatred and fears.

The only way to reclaim the treasure chest is to reclaim your power. You need to feel the rush and surge of your soul energy and embrace it in all its glory. To truly embrace your soul, you have to love yourself. You have to love yourself undoubtedly and unwaveringly and accept everything about yourself—mind, body, and soul. When you love yourself on this level, the treasure chest will be revealed to you. When you love yourself, the contents of the treasure chest will make sense to you.

THE BENEFITS OF SELF-LOVE

The quickest and simplest way to start operating your life from a place of positive energy and connection with the Universe is to ask yourself one question: "What is the most loving thing I can do for myself right now in my current situation?" And then go and do it. The first answer that pops into your mind is a great place to start when it comes to learning how to love yourself.

Listen to Your Own Advice

One of the easiest ways to start treating yourself with love is to think about someone you love. How do you treat this person? If this person were in the same situation as you, what advice would you offer them? The advice you give this person is the same advice you should take for yourself.

Every issue or complication in your life can be traced back to a lack of self-love on a deeper level. On the other hand, when you love yourself, you will:

- Find it very difficult to tolerate experiences in your life that are unsupportive or negative.
- Make it your number one priority to find solutions so you can feel at peace and in balance with yourself.
- Have the power to understand that everything in life is always unfolding perfectly and for your highest good.
- Feel supported by the Universe and supported by life. This is a very powerful feeling and is what will give you the strength and faith to live the life of your dreams.
- Change the relationship that you have with the world. Relationships that no longer serve you seem to melt away, and the way

you see the world also shifts to a more loving and supportive place.

- Open up room for the Universe to bring love into your life in the form of experiences and people.

If you don't love and accept yourself, how can you expect other people to do the same? If you don't love and accept yourself, how can you expect the Universe to show you the potential that lives inside? You cannot live a life of joy and happiness if you don't love yourself. Start loving yourself by practicing loving thoughts toward yourself and treating yourself in the same way you would treat someone you love.

When you start to treat yourself as a loved one, rather than as an enemy, when you start to watch what you say to yourself and start supporting yourself, you create a greater sense of joy and happiness. It also allows you to start opening yourself and your heart out to the Universe.

THINK ABOUT HOW YOU TALK TO YOURSELF

Your inner dialogue with yourself is incredibly powerful. It is the foundation for your life and it is the foundation of your energetic vibration. When you can speak to yourself lovingly and gently, you build your life on a solid foundation. When you hate yourself, when you are harsh or rude to yourself, it makes it very difficult to find the confidence to go after your dreams and build a life that feels loving and joyous.

Unfortunately, self-love doesn't come naturally to many of us. Chances are you will have to learn how to love yourself and practice it daily.

Exercise: Learning to Love Yourself

The first step to loving yourself is to monitor your thoughts and watch whenever you say anything mean or hurtful to yourself. When you notice these thoughts, try to switch them to something more positive. Even if you made a mistake or did something that you are feeling regretful for, be gentle with yourself and remind yourself that it will all work out as it needs to. Perhaps even write a positive affirmation or message to yourself that you can repeat whenever you feel negative thoughts arising. Here is an example to get you started: *"I embrace and love all that I am. I accept myself for all that I am. I am love."*

Another way to feel the energy of self-love is to look at yourself in a mirror (completely naked works best!) and repeat, *"I love you."* At first, you may not believe it, and the words may feel difficult or strange to say. But the more you can practice this, the more you are going to feel love radiating from the inside out.

CHOOSING POSITIVE THOUGHTS

Hand in hand with speaking to yourself kindly is choosing positive thoughts. You do indeed have the power to choose your thoughts. That's right—you can choose your thoughts, just like you would choose a pair of shoes or the clothes you wear. In fact, by choosing thoughts that are aligned with the voice of your soul, you can create a life that is filled with positive energy.

Choosing positive thoughts takes practice, but eventually it will come naturally to you. In order to start choosing your thoughts, you need to take inventory of your mind. Think of your thoughts like a grand buffet that is laid out in front of you. Depending on your mood or the events of your life, you are going to be drawn to different thoughts, just like you are drawn to various foods at the buffet table. Everything at the buffet is accessible to you, but you want to choose only the foods that are going to satisfy your cravings and fill you up. There may be foods at this buffet that you don't like or that you don't want. You don't have to engage with those foods, you can simply pass them up for something else. You can simply reach for another item of food that is more to your liking and is going to make you feel good.

Your thoughts work in a very similar way. You can think whatever you want, but choosing thoughts that are going to lift you up and make you feel good about yourself are obviously going to help you tune in to a more positive place of being.

When you get caught up in negative thinking or in a thought that doesn't feel good, it can be very hard to stop and break the cycle. But you can do it. Before you run away with the negative thought, clear your mind and reach for something else. Give yourself permission to ditch the negative thought and reach for something more delicious and satisfying. This habit takes awareness and practice, but the more you become aware of negative thoughts and the more you replace them with something positive, the easier it will be for you to operate from this place all the time.

Exercise: Switching a Negative Thought for a Positive One

It is challenging to know how to switch your thoughts. When you are first starting out, try choosing the opposite thought to the negative one you are having. For example, if you find yourself saying "I am so dumb," replace it with "I am smart at many things." If you find yourself saying "Nothing ever works in my favor," replace it with "Things are always working in my favor." Even if you don't believe the positive statement right away, the more often you choose positive thoughts, the easier it is going to be for you to believe them.

Practice being aware of your thoughts over the next fourteen days and replace any negative thoughts with positive ones. Over time, it will become easier to believe your positive thoughts, which in turn will help you to start feeling good.

SELF-LIMITING BELIEFS

Any resistance you have to loving yourself wholeheartedly is due to self-limiting beliefs. A self-limiting belief is essentially fear, in some form or another. It might be a fear of:

- Not being good or worthy enough to live the life you desire
- Never having enough money
- Not being lovable
- Not being thin/pretty/fit enough
- Not being smart or talented enough
- Being alone, and so on

Fear can lower your vibration and separate you from accessing the amazing unlimited potential of your soul energy.

We all move through this life with self-limiting beliefs, and most of us don't even realize it. In fact, it is not until you awaken and start monitoring the constant chatter of your mind that you start to realize the self-limiting aspects of your inner dialogue.

When you start to identify any fears or self-doubts you are holding on to, you can instantly start challenging those beliefs, which will then change the way that you see things.

You Can Absorb Others' Thoughts

Some of us even walk around with thoughts in our heads that are not even ours. We collect beliefs along the way from people, family members, and experiences and hold on to them as if they belong to us. In fact, most of us have a labyrinth of thoughts that run through our mind, and many of these thoughts run against or are not conducive to the lives we really want to lead.

Often, we are our own worst enemy in our quest to live a positive life. We hold super high expectations for ourselves that cause us to feel worthless or trap us in our fears. In fact, most of us walk through life unaware that we are operating from a place of fear rather than love. We walk through life shackled to the worries and anxieties we have fabricated in our own minds. Most of us never actually stop to question where our thoughts truly come from and why we think the way that we do.

Exercise: Identifying Your Self-Limiting Beliefs

The hardest part of removing self-limiting beliefs is identifying them. If you have operated with a particular belief system for many years, it can be very difficult to peel back the layers and identify these fears. Here is an exercise that can help: Write a brief answer to one or more of the following questions. (Hint: if you are not sure which question to answer, go with the last one!)

1. If you suddenly found an unlimited amount of money in your bank account, what would you do differently in your life?
2. What would your dream body look like? Be sure to describe how it would feel to have your dream body. Would you do anything differently if you had this ideal figure?
3. Imagine that you are living your dream life. What would your life look like? How would you feel differently about waking up every day?

All these questions are designed to help you reflect back to where self-limiting beliefs may be operating in your life and what is holding you back from truly living a life that feels good to you. Once you have finished answering the question(s), reflect back on what you have written and ask yourself, "What is stopping me from achieving all of this *now*? Is it really money, or is it something deeper? Is it truly a perfect body, or is it something deeper?"

Often the things stopping you are just excuses that can easily be overcome through a shift in your mindset. It can be tempting to think that all your problems are simply going to vanish when you acquire more money, get that perfect body, and so on. But this tempting thought is actually another self-limiting belief that will keep you trapped in fear. Take the time to go through your answers and see what feel-good emotions were stirred in you during the process. Think about how you can generate these feel-good emotions in your life right now.

If you want to change your life, if you want to feel love radiating from the top of your head to the tips of your toes, you have to break past these self-limiting barriers. You have to find the magic of your soul that was given to you and reclaim it. The only way you can do that is to come face to face with your fears.

REPROGRAMMING SELF-LIMITING BELIEFS

When you have operated with a self-limiting mindset for a long time, it can be challenging at first to switch over to a line of thinking that is more loving and abundant. In order to embrace the idea of self-love, you need to learn to speak to yourself in an entirely different voice. It's almost like learning a new language! Instead of putdowns, sighs of resignation, and shrugs, teach yourself more productive, abundant responses to the challenges you face. Here are some ideas.

Self-Limiting Beliefs in Action	Loving Beliefs in Action
When life throws obstacles my way, I feel like a victim. Everything is always working against me. It makes me feel better to complain, but only temporarily.	Challenges are an opportunity for growth. Even though things may seem challenging or difficult right now, I am learning a lot and discovering new things about myself and others.
The world is a very competitive place and I know there is not enough for everyone. Only a select few can make it. I will never be able to get ahead in life, so why bother trying?	I am infinitely supported by the Universe and everything that needs to come my way will find me. There is enough for everyone in the Universe and I always get what is best for me at any given moment.
I am not worthy, or smart enough, or talented enough to pursue my real dreams. It is difficult to find a job in my dream field and money is hard to come by.	There is nothing holding me back from pursuing my dreams. There is always a solution to every hurdle, as long as I think with an open mind. Money is always flowing to me in all areas of my life.
I am afraid of what other people will think of me. I constantly feel the need to say yes to others, so no one will be upset with me.	I value other people's opinions but I stay true to my own heart and do what is best for me, regardless of what others may say.
I feel jealous when other people find success or get what I want. I define my success by how successful other people think I am.	I rejoice in other people's successes and view success in my own terms. Success is a mindset more than an external place of being.

When you start operating your life from a more loving mindset, it automatically helps you to shed self-limiting beliefs and raise your energetic vibration. If you notice a self-limiting thought arising for you, try seeing if you can switch it to a more loving thought and see how that changes your outlook. At first you will need to put some effort into doing this, but over time it will come to you naturally and organically.

Exercise: Practicing Gratitude

Expressing gratitude is the quickest and easiest way to shift your vibration to a place of love. At the end of every day, take a moment to reflect on five things that you feel grateful for. Really allow yourself to *feel* the gratitude radiating from your being, as this will help to raise your energy levels. Gratitude is one of the most powerful forces in the Universe, and all of us have something to be grateful for, no matter how bleak life may seem. For best results, practice this exercise every day for 30 days.

CHAPTER WRAP-UP

Self-love is the most healing and powerful thing you can do for yourself. When you learn to love yourself deeply, and tame your self-limiting beliefs, everything else will begin falling into place, almost as if by magic. When you love and honor yourself, you will feel guided, supported, and nourished no matter what life brings your way. This in turn will allow you to find the freedom to be who you truly are and act from a place of pure authenticity—from the place of your soul.

- You already have everything you need to create a life that feels good from the inside out. Once you realize this, you can begin to access this power and shift your life to a more inspired and positive place.
- Learning to love yourself is the most valuable and important thing you can do for yourself. Treat yourself with kindness, embrace and love all that you are, and speak to yourself in a loving and gentle way.
- You can choose to have positive thoughts. With practice you will begin to believe your positive thoughts, and they will come to you naturally.
- When you practice thinking loving and abundant thoughts, it makes it very difficult for fear to hold you back. You'll find it easier to go after your wildest dreams.
- When you learn to identify self-limiting beliefs and switch them into something more loving, it shifts your energy to a more positive and loving vibration so you can attract more of what you want.
- Once you love yourself, everything else falls into place.

PART 2

Working with the Energy of the Universe

CHAPTER 4

YOUR CREATIVE POWERS

You are a creative being who is here to take the stardust from your fingertips and turn it into art for the world, for yourself, and for the Universe.

TAPPING INTO YOUR CREATIVE POWERS

We live in a highly creative Universe and a highly creative Universe lives within us. The Universe is always expanding and life is always being created through us and around us. We are part of this creative process and we have the ability to co-create the shape of the Universe.

As an energetic being, your creative powers begin with your energetic vibration and frequency. At any given time, your vibrations are being sent out into the Universe. It is these vibrations that allow the Universe to create. It is almost like the Universe takes all these collective vibrations from each and every one of us, and then manifests them into the world around us. Think of it like a piece of music: We each carry a different set of musical notes and together we all create the song of the Universe. We are collectively responsible for the world we are creating, and we can adjust what we create by focusing our energetic vibration on what we want rather than on what we don't want. Again, it all comes back to frequency: The more we can raise our vibration through positive thoughts, words, and actions, the more likely we are to create a life that reflects positive energy back to us.

The more you can understand your role as a co-creator, the more you will be able to have a say in what you choose to create. It is important to understand that while your energetic vibration does affect your reality, you are not in charge of everything that comes your way. The Universe itself, your soul, and the energy of the Divine also have a say in what you have been sent to experience. This is why you are a co-creator. We are all creating the Universe together as a team. Every living, breathing thing on this planet is helping to shape the world that we live in.

YOUR ROLE AS A CO-CREATOR

It may be difficult for you to comprehend that you are basically a ball of intensely powerful energy floating through the Universe in the shape of a human that has the ability to manifest and create things through your own energetic vibration. But when you see this in action for yourself, you will be able to understand it on a deeper level.

When you are operating from a higher vibration, life tends to reflect this back to you, just as when you are operating from a lower vibration, life tends to reflect this back to you as well.

High versus Low Vibrational Energies

Remember, higher vibrational energies include love, joy, laughter, abundance, gratitude, healing, miracles, and a sense of purpose. All of these vibrate at a higher frequency level as compared to lower vibrating energies, which include fear, anger, guilt, self-loathing, and lack of self-worth.

Lower vibrating energies are necessary for your growth and development so they do serve an important purpose. But when your vibration constantly operates from this place, it can be very difficult for you to attract positive experiences into your life. When you are focused on self-hatred, you only attract more of it. When you are focused on guilt or never being good enough, you only attract more of this energy.

Just the same, when you focus on abundance, you attract more of it. When you focus on joy, you attract more of it. It seems so simple . . . because it is. Your thoughts and feelings are powerful seeds of creation. When you radiate energy from your being, this energy is sent out into the Universe and becomes an energetic potential for creation. The more energy that is given to something, the more likely it is to manifest into your reality. This means that the more you focus on something and believe something, the more likely you are to see it showing up in your life. This is almost like a self-fulfilling prophecy. When you think something is going to happen, you almost start looking for it, expecting to see it, and waiting for it to arrive . . . and with the right energy and attention, it almost certainly does.

In order to tap into your creative powers, think about something you would like to create (starting with an emotion would be easiest), then start looking for examples of it in your life right now. Expect to see it more, know that it is coming, but more importantly allow yourself to really feel and believe it. Keep focusing your attention on this for the next few days and see what happens. You may be surprised at how quickly your creative powers are able to work.

A SUCCESSFUL RECIPE FOR CREATION

Creating in the Universe is almost like following a recipe. Just because you put certain ingredients together doesn't mean you are going to get the outcome you planned for. You could have followed the recipe word for word, but the end result is not always in your control. When it comes to the recipe for creation, it is not so much the outcome that you need to worry about or focus on, it's the ingredients that you are using. To use your powers as a co-creator effectively, you need to focus more on the ingredients than the end result.

Exercise: Your Creative Powers in Action

To see your creative potential in action, start by thinking about an event in your life that you wish to go smoothly. Perhaps you have an upcoming trip planned or a family gathering that you would like to go well. Perhaps you have even planted a new vegetable garden and want it to take off. Pick any event or situation in your life that has some meaning or significance to you.

Once you have chosen your event/situation, close your eyes and visualize how you would like things to go. Start seeing the most positive outcome and things going very smoothly. Imagine yourself feeling thankful and grateful for the happy outcome. If you notice any negative or self-limiting beliefs around the situation arising, allow them in but then see if you can switch them to a more abundant and positive mindset.

Keep repeating this exercise every day until the event arises, then sit back and watch what happens. Were you able to create the desirable outcome that you were looking for, even if there was just a small change?

This exercise shows how you can play a part in creating your reality. What you focus on in your mind begins to appear in your outer world. Your thoughts and feelings are truly magic, and the more you can utilize their power, the more you can be an active participant in the Universe that you live in.

These "ingredients" are the energetic vibrations that you need to emit from your being so you can create what it is that you desire. For example, if you want to create more love in your life, you need to radiate and feel the vibration of everything love means to you, such as passion, openness, compassion, freedom, and so on. You need to add all of these vibrations to the mixing bowl and feel them radiating through your being whenever possible. The stronger you feel these things on the inside, the more likely you are to create these things on the outside.

The most powerful way to use your creative powers is to generate feel-good emotions in your life. Think about an emotion that you would like to fill your life with—for example, joy. Focus on the feeling of joy for a moment, and perhaps even cut out pictures that make you feel full of joy. Keep these pictures close to you so you can look at them frequently. Over time, you will start noticing joy in your life, which will then allow you to create more joy too.

HOW YOUR THOUGHTS INFLUENCE YOUR REALITY

Many people struggle with the idea that thoughts play such a big role in the creation of their reality. If this was true, that would mean we are also responsible for the seemingly bad or negative experiences that come into our lives. Perhaps a better way to look at this would be, your thoughts create how you *perceive* your reality. Events are happening in our lives all the time, and it is our mindset (or vibration) that paints them as being negative or positive. In truth, there really is no such thing as negative or positive. Your reality is simply what you choose to focus on and how you choose to see things. Every experience is an opportunity to grow, and every experience offers both positives and negatives, depending on how you want to see it.

The more "positive" things you can focus on, the more positivity you will create in your life. It is that simple. Of course, you can focus on positive emotions all you like, but you genuinely also have to feel them. If life is challenging or is a struggle, it might be difficult for you to shift your focus onto something positive, but there is *always* something to be positive about. There is always something to be grateful for. Even if you just start small, that small shift can make all the difference.

NEGATIVE THOUGHTS AND CREATION

If your thoughts and vibrations help to shape your reality, then what do you do with negative thoughts when they arise? When you realize how powerful your thoughts are, it can be tricky to navigate through negative emotions. Of course, none of us want to be vibrating on a lower level, and none of us want to be creating or attracting negative experiences for ourselves. It is important to understand, however, that simply having negative emotions is not going to create negative or bad things in your life, although having negative thoughts and feelings will make it harder for you to deal with your life and the events that come your way. Thinking negatively or choosing self-limiting beliefs are always going to make it harder for you to create a life that feels rewarding and abundant.

Negative emotions are a fact of life, but when you hold on to them and wallow in them, they make it very, very difficult for you to create a life that feels positive and fulfilling. When you feel negative or self-limiting emotions arise allow them in, but then work on switching them to something more abundant and positive. Be as supportive to yourself as you can through this process and remember you are a co-creator. Your energy is only part of the picture. There are other forces at play as well, including the energy of the Universe, which is always supporting you and always lifting you higher. The Universe is always on your side. So even if you are going through a negative spell or struggling to keep yourself feeling positive, know that you are always being supported.

JUST BE YOURSELF

If you really want to be an effective co-creator in this world, then you need to be true to yourself. When your soul came into your body, it knew that everything about you was perfect. Your energy is exactly what the world needs and your energy is exactly what you came to give to the world. Everything we need is inside of us, which means in order to live the life that is truly destined for us, all we have to do is be ourselves. By simply being you, by freeing yourself from any labels, baggage, or heavy coats you may be wearing, you can release your energy into the world exactly as nature intended.

When you start being true to yourself and sending that energy out into the Universe, what you create and manifest back into your reality is also the best and most perfect match for you. Your only job in this life is to be you. When you radiate you, the Universe starts delivering experiences to you that are simply and purely aligned with your energy. This allows you to feel that you are one with life, and it also allows you to start walking the path of your highest purpose.

When you reach this place, you don't have to worry about whether your vibration is low or high, and you don't have to worry about the signals you are sending out to the Universe. You are automatically sending out and attracting the perfect experiences and reality for you.

Just be you.

Just be you.

Your Superpower

Your superpower in this life is that you are in control of your thoughts, words, and actions. Sure, these things can sometimes run away with you, but when you bring them back to your center, you can start becoming the alchemist. You can shift, flip, and clear your thoughts and emotions so they lift you up, inspire you to act, and create a life that makes you feel good.

At the end of the day, your life is what you make it. Every day holds 1,440 minutes that you can choose to live in joy or in fear. Every day, every minute, and even every second, is a chance for you to choose exactly what you want.

ALIGNING WITH THE PRESENT MOMENT

Staying present is the easiest way to join the flow of life. Joining the flow allows you to automatically create a life that is in vibrational harmony with your soul. When you are stuck in the past or always looking ahead to the future, it is impossible to sync with the creative energy of the Universe. In order to really align your vibration with the power of your soul, you have to bring your awareness to the now.

Being present doesn't mean that you can't ever *think* about the past or the future. Preparing for the future is great, as long as you are not trying to *live* in the future. There is a difference, and when you shift your awareness in this way, you reclaim your power and start working with the energy of right now.

> *"Welcome the present moment as if you had invited it. The present is all we ever have, so we might as well work with it rather than struggling against it. We might as well make it our friend and teacher, rather than our enemy."*
>
> —Pema Chödrön

When you start thinking about the future, often it can make you feel anxious or uncertain. Most of us are, in fact, not even aware of how much of our thinking is rooted in the future. We get anxious about the traffic on the way to work before we have even left the house; we get anxious about an upcoming meeting or date. Even small moments of anxiety keep us disconnected from the flow of the Universe. Returning your attention to the present, however, allows you to stay out of anxious energy and surrender to each moment as it comes. When you surrender to the now you accept the present moment and work with it, rather than against it.

Exercise: Be in the Present

Take a moment to identify seven things in the room that stand out to you right now. Doing this exercise brings your awareness into the present moment and allows you to merge your energy with that of the Universe. This simple exercise can be extremely powerful, and it can help you come back to the moment whenever you are feeling lost in thoughts of the past or future.

The future is simply a chain of events that you are contributing to in every moment. In order to create a bright future, your present also has to be bright. In order to create an abundant future, your present also needs to be rooted in abundant thinking. Every step you take is creating your future, so work on filling each step with the presence of now.

USING CREATIVITY TO CHANGE YOUR MINDSET

Just like we all have light within us, we also have darkness. Being in darkness usually brings about suffering, emotional pain, or feelings of misalignment. To some extent, this is all part of life but it is also very much a part of the creative process. Some of the most tortured souls have produced some of the most creative works of art. Perhaps even in your own life you have seen examples of how your own darkness has allowed you to create or birth something new.

CHANGING PERSPECTIVE

Being in a dark place in your life is usually a sign that you need to make a change. In fact, it is often the Universe's way of guiding you to approach things differently. A dark period can call you to change or create something new or different for yourself. Creation is often easier through suffering, as long as you can step outside of the suffering for a moment to realize this. While there is creative potential to this state of being, when you are in the midst of it, it's very difficult to see this.

Think of it like this. Imagine suffering as a big ball of dark energy. When you are caught up inside this big ball of energy, it is very difficult to see outside of it. All you know and all you feel is immense suffering and darkness. But when you free yourself so you can view this ball of suffering energy as an observer, you can see things in a new way and in a new perspective. It may even allow you to find a solution that perhaps you didn't realize was there.

This is what being in darkness does. Eventually the suffering becomes so hard to bear that it forces you to step outside of it and see it from a new perspective in order to change your life or change the way you view something. This change then gives fire to a new creative energy that allows you to create something new for yourself, be it a new set of circumstances or a new thought pattern.

CREATION AS THERAPY

When you are in a period of suffering, creative activities can sometimes be the best therapy. This is because making something shifts you into the creative mindset and gets you thinking about things in a different way. If you do find yourself feeling swept away into a period of darkness, try making time for creative activities, such as writing, drawing, dancing, singing, painting, and so on. What you create doesn't really matter, as the end result is less important than the creative process itself and what you feel while you are creating. Even just fifteen to thirty minutes a day of creative activity can be enough for you to start noticing the benefits.

Creation and Intuition

Activating the creative part of your brain also allows you to tap into more of your intuitive side, which may also help to bring clarity and understanding to your situation. It is the quiet, reflective moments that arise while you are creating that allow you to tap into that intuitive wisdom and hear the deeper calling of your soul.

BOOSTING PERSONAL GROWTH

When you feel lost, depressed, stuck, confused, or in pain, it is because you have outgrown the old and you need to create something new for yourself. You might be in this position because you need to sit with some feelings, or maybe because the Universe wants you to see something along your journey. Either way, suffering is part of the journey that your soul came here to experience in order to help you grow and rise up into the best version of yourself. Try to look at any "down" periods as having the potential to be amazing and positive periods of growth and change. If you can do this, perhaps these periods won't have such a heavy and weighted effect on your life.

> *"I wish I could show you, when you are lonely or in darkness, the astonishing light of your own being."*
>
> —Hafiz

When you can remember that suffering is really all about growth and change, then you can embrace all suffering with a newfound wisdom and understanding. You won't see suffering as a negative experience that is robbing you of your happiness, but as a time of growth that can help you shift to a new and even better place of being.

WHEN LIFE GOES LOW

We all have low points in our lives that are different depending on our journey or level of consciousness. Low points can sometimes bring us down and cause us to shift into depression, but again this is just a sign that growth and transformation are on the way. In fact, it is usually not until you have experienced your lowest points in life that you truly find the power to step up and take charge.

Traveling to these darker places and learning to transcend them allows you to see the potential in other people. Such experiences also allow you to deliver messages to others that are healing and inspiring. There is a beauty in the dark moments of life, and when we are able to embrace them and celebrate them as growing and learning experiences, then we loosen the grip of suffering and make life all the more peaceful.

Going Through Darkness in Order to Heal

In Native American and South American tribes, the shaman, who was the medicine doctor and healer for the entire village, had to go through a period of darkness and suffering in order to be initiated into the prestigious role of shamanic healer. Without being able to travel to such darkness, the shaman would not be able to be an effective healer. Likewise, without a similar journey we are not be able to truly understand the healing power and potential of our own body and mind. When we travel deep within ourselves and push past our own suffering into the light, we often become more positive. We may also gain a deeper understanding of other people and become more compassionate toward them.

CHAPTER WRAP-UP

You are a co-creator, which means that you are working with the energy of your soul, your environment, the Universe, and the life that is unfolding around you. You may not have control over everything that comes your way, but you do have control over how you handle what comes your way. You are in control of your feelings, thoughts, and emotions, and the more you can use these things to lift you up and inspire you, the more fulfilling and positive your life will become. This is the true nature of your creative powers.

- You are a co-creator in the Universe, and your creative powers start with the energetic vibration that you are sending out into the world.

- Your energetic frequency dictates what you have the power to create. So, to lead a positive life, focus on higher vibrational emotions, feelings, and thoughts.
- Your thoughts create your perception of reality. Therefore, you can change your thoughts to change your reality.
- Everything you need is inside of you, and to live the life that is truly destined for you, all you have to do is be yourself.
- You join the flow of life by staying in the present. Joining the flow creates a life that is in vibrational harmony with your soul. The more you can focus on being present and accepting each moment as an opportunity for growth, the easier it will be for you to live a life filled with ease and positivity.
- When we have low points in our lives, it is because we are getting ready to shift into a new level of high.
- Life is various shades of light and dark, so embracing both sides is all part of the process of living.

CHAPTER 5

DISCOVER YOUR PURPOSE

Your purpose is all around you. It lives in you, breathes through you, and dances alongside you. All you have to do is allow it to guide and show you the way.

UNDERSTANDING WHAT A PURPOSE REALLY IS

Want to find your purpose? You first have to find yourself. This is because your purpose is not outside of you, it is inside of you. Understanding who you are and your purpose go hand in hand; there is no beginning or end to these concepts. You are here to be you, to bring your energy and shine your light onto the world. This is your purpose and that is what the world needs from you.

Your Purpose Isn't a Career

It is a commonly held myth that your purpose needs to be a job title or label. But the truth is, your true purpose is to embrace all of who you are and to live from a place that feels authentic and good to you.

Your purpose is like a force of energy that comes up from inside of you and helps direct the course of your life. Because your purpose flows from within you, everything that is unfolding in your life now is part of your purpose. It is your purpose to breathe the air you just inhaled, to read the words you are reading, and to be exactly where you are currently in time and space. Everything you create in your life is part of your purpose.

"When you believe in your heart more than your head, your purpose just starts to become who you innately are and what you naturally do . . . So

next time you ask yourself, 'what is my purpose?' maybe the more important question to ask yourself and to answer through the heart is—what am I going to spend my time doing today?"

—Brian D. Evans

Many of us move through life hiding who we truly are and living from a place of fear and self-doubt. When you do this, it causes you to shift out of alignment with yourself and to accept a life that feels very limiting. If you feel out of touch with your purpose or that you are not living up to the fullest of your potential, it is because you are essentially out of touch with your true inner self. Every circumstance you find yourself in, however, is always designed to bring you back to you. No matter what is going on around you, know that everything is exactly how it needs to be. Perhaps whatever is unfolding around you now is meant to be this way to show you something, to guide you, or to teach you. Either way your purpose is you, so everything connected to you is therefore part of your purpose. Once you start understanding and recognizing that, you can begin to align with the authentic vibration of your purpose.

FIND YOUR PASSIONS

When you tap into your soul and your true authentic self, you are automatically aligned with where you are meant to be and what you are meant to be doing. The easiest and fastest way to get to this place is to start doing the things that you love to do, the things that make you feel most authentically you. When you allow yourself time every day to do the things that make you happy, it helps align you with a purpose that feels good. Your passions and the things that make you happy are so important. Your passions were given to you as a gift and are powerful signposts to the direction of your life.

Exercise: List 100 Things You Love Doing

If you are struggling to determine your passions, perhaps you need to rework your idea of what passion really means to you. Everyone has a different way of being passionate about something, and everyone expresses passion differently. To help you discover your passions, start by making a list of a hundred things that you love or that you love to do. This is a very powerful exercise that can get your soul and your vibration tuned to the power of love. When you are forced to write a hundred things, you must really stretch your heart in an effort to explore all the things that you love to do.

Start with simple things like "spending time with family" or "reading on rainy nights" and so on. Keep digging deeper until you have a hundred items on your list. Most people find that the items on the top of the list and the end of the list hold the most value, in that they are the strongest clues as to what makes them come alive.

We all feel passionate about something, and part of our job in this life is to identify these passions and act on them. You don't have to turn your passion into a full career and you don't have to just focus on one passion. But you do need to find a range of passions and things that you love to do and then make the time to do them every single day. When you allow yourself this freedom, you will:

- Feel aligned with the essence and vibration of who you really are.
- Have access to some guidance from the Universe as to what your soul has come here to learn, grow, teach, share, and experience.
- Shift your life in a new and powerful direction that is filled with joy, positivity, hope, and confidence.
- Find yourself filled with optimism and with the strength you need to make powerful and permanent changes in your life.
- Feel the power and potential of your soul energy and connected to the unconditional love that lives inside us all.

WHAT ARE YOUR NATURAL TALENTS?

Another important clue as to what your soul has come here to achieve is found in your natural talents. Is there something you are just naturally good at? Growing up, I had a friend who was an amazing singer. While she took singing classes, she also had a natural talent and flair for using her voice. Her voice was so beautiful and so powerful and so moving that it was hard to imagine that her voice had *not* been given to her for some higher purpose. Today, even though she didn't make a career out of singing, she uses her voice as a way to share her gifts with the world through public speaking and teaching. Everyone has natural talents; in fact, often these talents come so naturally to us that we are not really even aware of them as "talents." Maybe you are really good at using your hands, at cooking, or with animals. We all have talents and skills. Becoming aware of them can help you discover what you are meant to be doing in this life and what gifts your soul has come to share with the world.

Find Your Joy

When you get clear about what you feel passionate about and act on those things, even if it is just for a few moments every day, it allows you to instantly connect with your soul. Many of us make the mistake of thinking that life is supposed to be tough and challenging. While there is some truth to this at times, life is really about finding joy and doing things that make you feel alive. Ask yourself: What makes me feel alive? What makes me feel happy to be alive?

Your soul didn't go to all the effort of coming into physical form to simply live a boring existence; your soul came to live a life of passion and joy. And when you experience that every day, you can start to shift your life in a positive direction.

FOLLOW WHAT YOU LOVE: HOW I FOUND MY PURPOSE

When you listen to your heart and begin following what you love, everything else gradually begins to fall into place. My journey with this began around ten years ago after I had my first awakening. This awakening allowed me to understand that I had rivers of information living inside of me that needed to be released into the world. This feeling grew and grew, so as an outlet I started blogging to get these messages out into the world. I didn't have any plans or a goal; it just felt like the right thing to do. It was a slow start at best, and my blog received just a small handful of readers. I had no desire to be a writer or a blogger, so it didn't really bother me. I just did it because I felt called to write. At the time I was really passionate about being an actor in theater, film, and television. I felt so compelled to pursue this as a career that I turned my sights to Hollywood. I wanted to move to Los Angeles—I didn't know how that would happen; I just knew it would. And sure enough, all the way from Melbourne, Australia, I eventually landed on L.A.'s doorstep. I did the whole acting game and auditioned and so on. But after a while I started to grow tired of it. I stopped finding it fun and rewarding. Instead I felt stressed out and anxious all the time.

> *"I've come to believe that each of us has a personal calling that's as unique as a fingerprint—and that the best way to succeed is to discover what you love and then find a way to offer it to others in the form of service, working hard and also allowing the energy of the Universe to lead you."*
>
> —Oprah Winfrey

Eventually, I lost interest in acting and decided to take a break so that I could reconnect with myself and figure out what I wanted to do. During this time, I felt a host of emotions. Leaving acting made me feel like somewhat of a failure, almost like something inside of me had died. That flame, that passion I had for film and theater seemed to have just vanished into nothing. Then one fateful day, the very same day that I ended my agreement with my agent and manager, I met and became friends with an entrepreneur who specialized in creating websites and blogs. One day, embarrassed, I showed him my measly blog that I hadn't updated in years. He was amazed by the information, and he encouraged me to start blogging again to get my messages out there. I shrugged off his suggestions, but then, as if the stars had all aligned, I received a call out of the blue from an old friend I used to study with. He was in town and wanted to catch up. While catching up with him, he coincidentally shared an idea for a blog he wanted to start. It too would be about things relating to spirituality, healing, and mindfulness. We began chatting and before I knew it, we had agreed to create a blog together. That blog was ForeverConscious.com.

It started out small, but with some help and Divine guidance, the blog took off and started attracting more and more readers. I realized that there was such a thirst for this type of information and that this was a way that I could get my messages out in the world. I also started connecting with my readers in a deeper way, offering them intuitive readings and guidance. Through this process, I slowly started to feel my inner flame return, and I knew that even though I had moved to Los Angeles for acting, my journey was a whole lot bigger than just that.

If you have a dream or goal that you wish to turn into a reality, start small. Start by breaking your goal down into smaller, more managaeable ones and then work on achieving them step by step and day by day. Small progress like this can often add up to big results.

BELIEVE IN YOURSELF

One of the biggest things that stand in our way of going after our goals, dreams, and wishes is not having enough self-belief. Often we know what we like to do or what we wish we could be doing with our lives, but lack of confidence and low self-esteem gets in our way.

As you start raising your vibration, loving yourself, and aligning your life with positive energy, it will become easier to feel motivated and trust yourself in the pursuit of what you really want to be doing with your life. When you trust yourself and give yourself permission to go after your passions and talents, it allows you to feel more purposeful in your day-to-day life. It also gives you the courage to turn your passions into a career path.

Exercise: The Power of Believing in Yourself

When you trust yourself, when you believe in yourself, it will be a lot easier to go after your dreams and goals. When you are always second guessing yourself or doubting your abilities, it makes it impossible to succeed.

Start by using affirmations throughout the week that remind you to trust and believe in yourself. You can write your own affirmation, but here is one to get you started: *"I believe in myself and I trust myself. I know I am capable of pursuing my goals and that I will be able to handle whatever is sent my way. I know I can do anything when I believe in myself. I can do it!"*

The first step with pursuing any dream or goal, particularly as a career, is believing in yourself. This will allow you to overcome any obstacles and tame any fear that you may have. When pursuing a dream there is always the risk of failing. But failure is not necessarily a bad thing. Failure is simply an opportunity to learn, grow, and try again. Even though I moved to Los Angeles to pursue a career as an actor and failed, that doesn't mean that it wasn't a highly rewarding or positive experience. In fact, moving to Los Angeles was one of the best decisions I ever made! When you go after your dreams and passions, the end result may not be how you planned it to be, but it can lead you to even more incredible destinations that you never thought were possible. When you have a dream or a goal to achieve, believe in yourself, trust yourself, give yourself permission to succeed at it and fail at it, but most importantly, give yourself permission to at least try.

CHAPTER WRAP-UP

Your purpose is inside of you and flows through you; it is not something external. Your purpose is to be yourself, to be truly authentically you. This way of life brings you into alignment with your soul and allows you to naturally attract and discover your passions and talents.

- You already have access to your purpose, for it is inside of you. Everything that is unfolding in your life is part of your purpose.
- In order to feel aligned with your purpose, you have to first be aligned with yourself.
- Dedicating your time to your passions and the things you love to do can naturally raise your energy and align you with a more purposeful life.
- The things that you are naturally good at may provide clues as to where you should be focusing your energy and attention.
- Pursue your highest dreams and goals by believing in yourself and breaking down your goals into more manageable steps.

CHAPTER 6

LET THE UNIVERSE GUIDE YOU

You live in a powerful Universe and a powerful Universe lives inside of you. When you connect these two Universes together, true magic is born.

THE UNIVERSE IS ON YOUR SIDE

At the core of the Universe is a pure unconditional love that is so strong and so powerful that even the word "love" can't really capture it. This amazing, incredible, loving energy is the same energy that you were created from, and it lives and breathes inside this entire Universe and inside of you.

I can't say this enough: The Universe is always supporting you, always guiding you, and always protecting you.

When you learn to tap into the energy of the Universe, by following the signs that are presented to you and trusting that you will always be guided, you will see that life is always working in your favor and not against you.

At first, you have to program your mind to see the miracles of the Universe in action. You have to actively try to notice how and when the Universe is working in your favor. Unfortunately, most of us move through our lives completely unaware of how the Universe has always been guiding and protecting us.

HOW I KNOW THE UNIVERSE IS ALWAYS ON MY SIDE

Many years ago I won a United States green card in a lottery program. Moving to the United States was always something I wanted to do, so I packed my bags and left my home in Australia, for life in the USA. Before moving, I had set up accommodations through a friend of a friend. I didn't feel all that great about the deal, but I wanted to have something set up ahead of time. I had even paid rent and was ready to settle into my new home. After a long flight, I arrived at my new home only to find out that there really was no room and that the "friend" of my friend had taken my money and had no intention of giving it back or giving me a room.

Needless to say, I was upset—but this experience taught me an extremely valuable lesson that I cherish today. After checking myself into a hostel for the night, I fatefully met an Indonesian woman and I confided my story to her. She explained that money always has a way of coming back around, and that money truly doesn't belong to us anyway. It is simply an energetic current that is transferred from one person to another. She assured me that money lost always comes around in another form.

Several months later, when I had settled into a new residence, I still harassed this person to give me back my money, but all my efforts were in vain. Eventually the process was causing me so much stress and consuming so much of my time that I decided to let it go and trust the Universe. I decided to listen to what the lady in the hostel had shared with me and trust that the money would come back to me in even better ways. I even developed and recited a mantra: *"For every dollar I give away, three come my way."*

About one year later, long after I had let go of the money I was owed, I was at a party hosted by a good friend of mine, and of course, who did I bump into at this party? The person who had taken my money. I confronted him about the situation. He was extremely embarrassed because many of his work colleagues overheard what we were discussing. The next day, I received an envelope with the money in it that I was owed. The Universe sure does work in mysterious ways. This is just one of many events in my life that prove to me the Universe is always working in my favor.

Now, if you are wondering: "If the Universe is always on your side, why would you have lost this money to this friend of a friend in the first place? Where was the Universe for you then?" I am happy to tell you that the Universe was warning me. I had a strong intuition not to follow through with this arrangement, but my logical mind took over and assured me that I was just worrying for no reason. After all, I reasoned, he was a friend of a friend, and he could be trusted. I ignored my gut feelings and went ahead and did it anyway. At the end of the day, even though I ignored my instincts, the Universe got me where I needed to be.

WHEN SEEMINGLY BAD THINGS HAPPEN

While my story of losing some money is no big deal in the grand scheme of things, you may be wondering how the Universe can be on the side of people who are living in extreme poverty or in war-torn countries. To answer this question, you have to understand the Universe as a whole. At the center of the Universe is love. The soul of the Universe is love. Just the same, you have a soul and that soul is also love. Along with a soul you also have thoughts, energy, and a vibration that are sent out into the Universe. This energy and vibration help create the reality that we all live in and experience.

As a society, when we hold on to fears, anger, greed, and pain, we are collectively sending out these vibrations into the Universe, causing disharmony on earth. This disharmony and pain causes people to act in certain ways and to participate in crimes and in the disruption of peace on earth. Souls that cannot find peace within themselves cannot create a life that is centered on peace, and therefore these acts of suffering occur. It is important to understand that suffering doesn't happen because you have done something wrong or because you have bad karma. Suffering to some extent is part of what we have come here to experience in this life. While it is not fair or even necessary to measure suffering, because we all have our own issues that we are dealing with, it is important to understand why we suffer. Although it may be impossible to answer with certainty why we suffer, one thing is for sure: suffering always leads to growth.

THE UNIVERSE DOESN'T CAUSE SUFFERING; YOUR THOUGHTS AND FEELINGS DO

Seemingly bad things happen to good people all the time. It is important to understand however that "bad" is relative. What you initially perceive as being bad may end up being the best thing that ever happened to you. For example, you may feel that it is "bad" to get a divorce, and the first year after the divorce, you might feel an immense amount of suffering and pain. But as your life moves on, you may start to realize that getting divorced was a good decision that freed you up to make changes in your life. Over time, you may start to see the silver lining and how things needed to unfold the way they did for a greater cause or purpose. Perhaps you start to see how the timing and all the events that unfolded were actually perfect.

If you give yourself the ability to look at life this way, you are always going to have the tools and strength you need to breathe through your suffering rather than allowing it to consume you. Looking at life in big-picture terms also allows you to see the lesson that is unfolding and how the suffering is ultimately leading to an immense period of growth and development. It also allows you to see your life as a perfect sequence of events that is always unfolding as it is meant to unfold.

Exercise: Getting to the Root of Your Suffering

Because suffering is usually a product of your mind, in all likelihood your suffering will be linked to both your conscious and subconscious thoughts. Identifying your conscious thoughts isn't too difficult. But what about those subconscious thoughts? The subconscious mind is programmed and filled with repetitive tapes and belief systems that you have collected since your first day on earth. As you can imagine, most of us have a subconscious mind that is clogged with a host of buried thoughts, feelings, and emotions from our past. In order to start clearing the toxic thoughts of your subconscious mind and unearthing your skeletons, you must first identify them. A journaling exercise developed by author Julia Cameron is one of the simplest and most effective tools you can use for doing this.

Here is how it works. Keep a notepad and pen by your bedside. Every morning when you wake up, before you do anything else, write three to four full pages, back and front, about anything that comes to your mind. You can write down thoughts, feelings, events, whatever you like. The trick is to keep writing without pausing or taking a break. If you don't know what to write, make it up or write gibberish—just keep writing until you have completed three to four double-sided pages. Repeat this exercise every morning for thirty days for maximum benefit.

At the end of the thirty-day period, you will have a journal filled with some of your deepest subconscious thoughts that you probably were never even aware existed. Having these thoughts out on paper can be extremely healing and enlightening, and they can point you in the direction of the deeper subconscious thoughts behind your suffering. When looking back over your writing, try to identify patterns in an effort to discover what thoughts may be contributing to your suffering.

The tricky thing about suffering is that it's not usually the actual event that makes you suffer; instead, it is your thoughts and feelings about the events that causes the suffering. Something unfortunate may happen, but if you look at it objectively, you can recognize that the event is already over. It is your emotions and your mind that keeps the event alive and causes you to enter into suffering. Feelings of guilt, anger, embarrassment, remorse, and a host of other emotions can all add to your suffering.

If you want to be released from the claws of suffering, you have to first address the thoughts in your mind and bring stillness, acceptance, and love to what you are feeling. After you have allowed yourself to accept and process all the emotions you are feeling, you can truly transcend your suffering. When you hold on and refuse to let go, the claws of suffering will forever have you in their grips.

When you learn how to identify the fundamental causes of your suffering, it is a lot easier to move past them. Make no mistake, this is a lot easier said than done. Start by observing your thoughts, especially any repetitive thoughts, and you will begin to unearth the roots of your suffering. More often than not, the roots are also much deeper than you realize.

CAN YOU SAVE OTHERS FROM SUFFERING?

As a healer and intuitive reader, my job is to help people process their suffering. Through this, I have come to realize two things:

1. You cannot save everyone.
2. Suffering is your greatest teacher, as long as you are able to identify your suffering.

When it comes to helping people through their suffering, the most beneficial thing you can do is to listen without judgment. Create a safe space so people can feel comfortable enough to freely express what is truly bothering them. If they ask for advice, you can share some suggestions, but don't force them on the person. Even if the solution seems obvious to you, sometimes it is hard for others to see through all of their suffering. Gently guide them, but don't force them to see something they may not be ready to see.

Many years ago when I was first starting out on my journey as an intuitive, I met a woman who was very depressed and closed off from her soul. She had an affair more than twenty years earlier that had caused her marriage to end. During the breakup of her marriage, she felt immense remorse and regret, but her husband wouldn't take her back. After the divorce was finalized, the husband moved on with his life and started another family. She, on the other hand, had spent twenty years reliving the events over and over in her mind. She beat herself up and blamed herself, hating herself for the mistake that she made. She had spent thousands and thousands of dollars over the years speaking to psychics and healers, trying to find some peace.

When I gently pointed out to her that she needed to let her ex-husband go and move on with her life, she point-blank refused. Her response was something to the effect of, "I can't and I won't." It was just too painful for her to let him go. I gave her a few exercises to complete, but everything she tried was met with resistance. Needless to say, she didn't make much progress throughout her sessions. As a healer this was not the result I was hoping for, but this challenging client taught me a very valuable lesson: It is not your job to "save" people.

Sometimes, try as you may, there is very little you can do if the person you are helping is not ready to let go, step up, and take responsibility for his or her life. We all know the saying, "You can lead a horse to water, but you can't make it drink." That is a wise thing to remember, whether you are a healer or not. It can be hard to remember this or feel at peace with this idea when the person suffering is someone you love dearly. But often the best and most loving thing you can do is stand back, offer support from a distance, and only intervene when asked or when your intuition calls on you to do so. The rest you have to entrust to the hands of the Universe and believe that the person will figure it out in their own time and when they are ready.

PROOF YOU LIVE IN A MAGICAL UNIVERSE: THE LAW OF ATTRACTION AND INTENTION

Even though there is suffering in the Universe, there is also a lot of magic. No matter how bad or chaotic your suffering may be, at the end of the day things have a miraculous way of working out. Sometimes you may not always be able to appreciate the journey. But when it is over and you've had some time to reflect, you will find that there is always a reason for everything, and you'll see that the pieces of the puzzle will have fallen into place. Learning how to accept the journey without trying too hard to understand it allows you to see life as a magical journey of discovery, growth, and opportunity.

The Universe is showing us examples of its magic all the time. We have all had the experience of thinking about someone then seeing or hearing from that person moments later. We have all seen the amazing colors that light up the dusk sky during a sunset. We have all experienced the amazing healing power that lives inside all of us that allows our skin to heal from a cut and allows our bodies to regenerate as we sleep.

WHAT IS THE LAW OF ATTRACTION?

Your thoughts are energy signals, meaning that you can send out particular signals in order to attract things into your life. This process is commonly referred to as the law of attraction, and it is one of the most powerful laws in the Universe. The law of attraction has been used for centuries and is the art of using your thoughts to manifest your intentions into realities. Because the Universe is responding to the energy you are sending out, all you have to do is visualize what you want to create, really feel it and see it in your mind's eye, and then release it out to the Universe. This is a powerful exercise that can be used to attract things into your physical reality.

You can ask the Universe to send you a particular event or experience such as a new job or meeting a soulmate or even a physical item such as money or a car. Visualizing the *having* of the experience or the item, and sending signals out into the Universe, can help to manifest the experience into your life.

Exercise: Set an Intention

This is a visualization exercise you can try to help you see the power of the Universe in action. To do this, all you need to do is set an intention about what you want the Universe to show you. For example, you could ask the Universe to show you a sign or to deliver you a message about a particular situation in your life. State your intention clearly, and perhaps even put a reasonable timeframe on it or ask the Universe to show you the sign a number of times so you can be sure that you will notice it when it arrives.

To send out your request, really feel it and see it in your mind's eye. Visualize the Universe responding to your request and send your feelings out strongly and confidently. Then, thank the Universe for delivering your request and stay open-minded so you can be sure to hear the answer. I have used this exercise many times and I can say without a doubt that the Universe always answers.

HOW TO SET AN INTENTION

While managing your vibration and energy is one way to tap into the amazing potential of the Universe, another way is to set an intention. Intentions are like requests or declarations. Magically, the Universe always seems to respond to them. Setting intentions is not about having your every wish catered to; instead, it is about trusting that the Universe will take care of you by bringing you the best possible outcome. Intentions also help you clarify what you want and need from your life at any given moment, which can help give your life more direction and guide you to taking the best appropriate action.

THE UNIVERSE ALWAYS ANSWERS

The Universe is always working in magical ways, and the more open you can become to this the more you are going to see it. In fact, once you start becoming aware of it, you will begin seeing it all the time. Just yesterday a friend called me wondering if she should end a contract with a client that she had been working with. My friend is a graphic designer and while she appreciated the money and the business from this client, she had worked for them for many years and wanted to free up her time to welcome in something new. After our chat, she set an intention to the Universe and asked for clarity about what path she should take. In the morning she woke up to find an email from the client informing her that they would like to end their contract at the end of the month. The Universe had heard her intention and had taken care of the decision for her, allowing her to see the path that she was meant to take.

WHEN THE LAW "DOESN'T WORK"

Many people have used this technique and seen amazing success . . . but many people have also used this technique and seen nothing. What's the difference? This technique won't work if you have blocks surrounding the receiving of the energy, or if your ego gets involved and essentially demands things. And sometimes we don't really know what we want to create or what experiences are even best for us, so our intention is more cloudy than clear.

Here's an example. You may *think* you want a million dollars, but actually you just want security. You may *think* you want that new car, but actually you are just chasing status. When you use the law of attraction to ask for material items or possessions that are out of alignment with your soul, it often doesn't work or you end up missing something that could satisfy what you really need.

Exercise: Discover the Feelings Behind Your Intentions

In order to be sure your intentions match your vibration, you need to figure out what feelings are tied to your intention. For example, let's say you want to manifest the perfect job. First, think about the feelings that having this perfect job is going to create in your life. These feelings are more important than the *having* of the job itself, so start there. Make a list of all the feelings that having this job will bring for you, and then highlight two or three main ones that stand out to you. Let's say you choose freedom, financial security, and inspiration. Now, try to create these feelings in your life. Notice them when they appear, and be grateful for these feelings whenever they show up.

Shifting your awareness in this way allows you to have your "perfect job" now because you will feel a similar vibration. This allows your vibration to match what you want, and eventually, through Divine timing, that job will come your way.

Using the law of attraction is a great way to start experimenting with the power of the Universe, but it really is just the tip of the iceberg. You can send your wishes out into the Universe all you want, but the fact remains that the Universe is only going to send you experiences that match your vibration. Even if you ask for that perfect lover or that perfect job, if your vibration doesn't match the having of that thing, it will never come your way. Matching your vibration is really about matching what having that item means to you on an emotional level.

WHAT CAN YOU ASK THE UNIVERSE ABOUT?

There are no restrictions on what you can ask the Universe for guidance on. In fact, one of my favorite things to ask the Universe for is a parking spot. Living in a big city, parking can be tough at times and so before I arrive at my destination, I send a request out to the Universe for the perfect parking spot. I don't stress and obsess over how the Universe is going to send me this perfect parking spot, I simply just surrender, thank the Universe, and trust that my request will be heard. Every time, almost like magic, there is the perfect open parking spot waiting for me when I arrive.

Asking the Universe for help with the small things is sometimes a great place to start, but you can also ask the Universe to guide you on bigger and more important matters. I asked the Universe for guidance on moving from Los Angeles to a new city, for example. I had traveled to the city with the intention of looking at apartments and to get a real feel for the place. I held my intention in my heart and asked the Universe for a very clear and obvious sign whether moving to this city was a step in the right direction. On my first day there, however, I came down with food poisoning that seemed to come from out of the blue. I couldn't even make it to any of the apartments that I had scheduled to see and spent the entire night on the bathroom floor at the hotel! The next day when I was feeling slightly better, I abandoned my trip and headed back home to Los Angeles. When I got home I felt so happy and grateful to be back at my own place that in an instant, all my desires surrounding the move subsided. Funnily enough, when I got home, all traces of the "food poisoning" also magically vanished and I felt perfectly fine. Even though being sick was no fun, I took it as a very clear and obvious sign from the Universe.

Now, could getting sick have just been a coincidence? Of course. But the feeling I had when I got home felt so strong and so significant that I just couldn't help but feel this was the obvious sign that I had asked for.

Perhaps now that you are hearing my stories of how the Universe has guided me, you may be remembering some of your own. Was there ever a time in your life when you felt guided by the Universe?

SIGNS FROM THE UNIVERSE

In the beginning, it can be hard to interpret and see the signs of the Universe. But with patience and an open mind, you will soon realize that the Universe is indeed responding to you. In fact, the Universe is always sending you signs and looking out for you, even if you don't ask it to. Signs from the Universe can be very soft and subtle, such as a butterfly that lands on your shoulder or a cricket that sits on your doorstep. Or the signs can be a lot louder, like an unexpected circumstance that turns your life upside down.

Some of the most common signs from the Universe include:

- A random encounter with an animal that seems prophetic
- Chance encounters with people who seem to deliver timely messages or change the course of your day in some way
- Seeing repeated number sequences throughout the day
- Hearing or reading a message that seems to come at the right time
- Synchronistic events that are too uncanny to just be coincidences
- A disruption or cancellation to plans or meetings that seem to come from out of the blue
- Meeting people who you feel a strong reaction to or who remind you of someone from your past
- Constantly coming up against roadblocks or hurdles that seem to hold you back or delay you
- Losing or breaking a possession
- Falling sick repeatedly
- Seeing a leaf or flower drop on your path in a prophetic way (the type of flower may also hold a special significance to you that could add to your message)

The meaning of these signs will be unique and different depending on what is going on for you at the time they are being experienced. But tuning in to the messages the Universe is trying to send you can help you along your path. There are really no "wrong turns" in this life; you are simply here to grow and learn. The Universe is here for you to learn from, so why not use it to make your life easier?

BEING OPEN TO THE UNIVERSE

When you start developing a connection with the Universe, you can use it to help you manifest things in your physical reality. In order to develop a connection with the Universe, you first have to trust it. This means that you need to recognize when the Universe is guiding you and when the Universe is responding to the energy that you are sending out.

The Universe is always sending you signs; the trick is to be open to receiving them. A friend told me a story about a friend of hers who was upset because her son was getting married to a woman she did not approve of. She had tried talking with her son, begging him to reconsider, but he was in love and had made up his mind. The woman continued to fight against her son's decision and became even angrier when her family didn't support her. Everyone else in her family had accepted the son's decision and simply wanted him to be happy, whereas she continued to feel angry and frustrated. One day, she went for a walk with my friend and said that all she wanted was a sign that everything was going to be okay. At that moment, a white rose fell from a bush and landed right at her feet. She stopped to pick up the white rose, which is a symbol of peace and serenity, and instantly she felt a calming energy wash over her. In that moment, she had a resounding feeling that everything was going to be okay.

The Connection Between the Stars and You

The formation of the Sun, stars, Moon, and planets is also a sign from the Universe. These celestial bodies have been guiding us for eons, from the planting time of crops to the celebration of the new year. We all know the famous story of the three wise men who followed the special star to find the baby Jesus. Astrology is not a science but the study of the relationship between life on earth and life up above. Many people look to the planets and astrological signs for guidance, and many people feel the planets affecting their energy and mood. In astrology it is believed that "as above, so below," which means that because we are all part of the Universe, all planets and stars in a way are all part of us and therefore affect us. As a practicing astrologer myself, I am always blown away when I see the synchronicities between what the planets are doing and what is going on in my own life and the lives of those around me. In fact, on my website ForeverConscious.com, my astrology articles about the planets and the different cycles affecting us are always the most popular and generate the most attention.

HOW NATURE IMPACTS YOUR ENERGY

All matter in the Universe is made up of the same energy, which means that whatever is happening in nature is also reflected back within you on an energetic level. This is part of how everything is connected and is why you will sometimes feel the effects of nature on a spiritual level. For example, who hasn't been moved by stunning scenery and Mother Earth's beauty or felt the desire to curl up with a hot drink and a book on a frosty winter day?

THE LOST CONNECTION WITH MOTHER EARTH

Many years ago, our ancestors looked to Mother Earth for answers and direction. They looked to the Sun to determine the time of day and the seasons; they looked to the Moon to determine the tides of the oceans. They looked to the behavior of animals to predict natural disasters, and they tracked the weather as messages from the gods. Our ancient ancestors believed that Mother Earth was not a possession but a home that gave life and sustenance to all living things. They understood their lives through the eyes of nature, and this knowledge helped them survive and evolve.

Nature Is Healing

Mother Earth has historically played an important role in human culture, but in recent years, many of us have lost touch with this power. Spending time in nature has been proven to reduce stress and help stimulate the body's natural healing process, so be sure to get quality time outside every day!

HOW THE CYCLES OF NATURE IMPACT YOUR ENERGY

When you start paying attention to your natural environment, you can see the effect that the cycles and rhythms of nature have on your mind, body, and spirit. Notice how:

- In the months of spring, everything is in bloom and the energy of new life, creativity, and creation is high. All around you, new life is emerging and if you allow yourself to join in this rhythm and flow, perhaps you will also feel your own creative juices become stronger.
- In the summer months, your energy is often high and there is a strong desire to get out and do things. Many people take vacations during the summer months and spend time recharging their batteries under the energy of the Sun.
- In the months of autumn, the leaves start shedding and animals prepare for the winter. Perhaps you too feel this energy of release and surrender to it. Autumn might remind you to allow the dead things to drop away so you can prepare for something new.
- In winter, your energy is often lower and there is a desire to stay inside or go within. There is perhaps also a desire to reflect and restore yourself in order to prepare for the new beginning of spring. You might also be drawn to warming, nourishing foods, and life may move at a slower pace.

Nature often provides clues as to what is happening energetically in the Universe and inside of you. These clues help you to know which way you should be directing your energy. When you can sync yourself with the rhythm of nature, often it allows you to feel part of something bigger than just yourself and deeply connects you to the earth and to the Universe.

Exercise: Earthing

Whenever you are feeling off balance or out of touch with nature, here is a great exercise you can do to help bring you back into alignment with the energy of Mother Earth. This is also a great exercise to do when you are feeling stressed out or scattered, energetically speaking. Simply take off your shoes and socks and walk barefoot on the grass for fifteen minutes. This practice is called Earthing, and it allows the energy of Mother Earth to travel through your body and restore your energy and vibration. It will also help you to feel more grounded and connected with yourself and with the planet.

TUNING IN TO THE ABUNDANCE OF THE UNIVERSE

There is enough in the Universe for everyone. There is no such thing as lack, and there is enough for everyone to get exactly what they need. You are not in competition with anyone else and no one can take what is truly yours. We are all on our own journey, and each of us is equipped with everything we need to live the life of our dreams. When you tune in to this mindset, you also tune in to the vibration of abundance. Acting from a place of abundance allows you to shift into the realm of infinite possibilities. When you think abundantly, nothing is impossible and everything is possible.

ABUNDANT THOUGHTS BRING EXPANSION AND SOLUTIONS

Abundant thinking can be as simple as saying "yes, I can" when you hear the voice of doubt creeping into your mind. Thinking abundantly also allows you to believe in yourself and in your abilities to succeed. Through abundant thinking, you will become aware of how life is always unfolding in your favor.

When you focus on a seemingly negative event that occurs in your life, you narrow your mindset and cause yourself to see things from a place of narrowness and scarcity. But when you expand your thinking into abundant thoughts, solutions appear because you see the larger plan at play.

DON'T LIMIT YOURSELF ENERGETICALLY

When you view life through a narrow window, you limit your creative ability and your ability to receive energy. If you want to fill your life with positive energy, you need to be ready and willing to receive that energy. You have to be ready and willing to take the energy inside you and match it up with the energy that you want to create outside of you.

Money is a perfect example of this. Think of money as an energetic current or currency that is exchanged around the world. If you want to receive energy or money, you have to open yourself to receive it. You cannot receive from a limited mindset; you can only receive from an abundant mindset.

> *"The fastest way to bring more wonderful examples of abundance into your personal experience is to take constant notice of the wonderful things that are already there."*
>
> —Esther Hicks

Therefore, in order to attract more money and energy into your life, you have to start opening yourself to abundant thinking and to the realm of infinite possibilities. When you are open to this point, money and energy starts flowing into your life in all ways.

Exercise: Opening Yourself to Abundance

In order to open to the abundance of the Universe, start paying attention to the many abundant blessings in your life. Make it a point to identify five blessings every single day, from your weekly paycheck to the amazing gift of the Sun. When you start recognizing abundance in your life, you are also creating space and room for more.

For every beat of energy that you give out into the Universe, you will always receive back three times as much, as long as there is space for you to receive it. Do you know how many times the Universe tried to send you something but you didn't believe you were worthy of it, so it stopped short of you? Open yourself to receiving, know that you are worthy, and know that you deserve to have a life filled with joy and abundance. But know that in order to create these things in your external world, you first have to feel them in your internal world.

CHAPTER WRAP-UP

You live in an abundant, ever providing, super magical Universe that is there for you to use and work with. The Universe is always sending you signs to help point and guide you in the right direction. The more you can tune in to this and trust this, the more you will start to see the magical forces of the Universe operating in your life.

- We live in a magical Universe of energy that is always responding to our vibration and guiding us to grow.
- Your thoughts, feelings, and vibration are powerful creators and play a vital role in how you engage with the Universe.
- Your energy and your thoughts can manifest things into your physical reality, but no matter how hard you "think" about what you want, you can only ever attract things that align with who you truly are.
- The Universe is always guiding you, and the more you can trust the signs and synchronicities of your environment, the more supported you are going to feel.
- Nature is always sending you clues about the energy that is around you and often guides you where you should be focusing your attention.

CHAPTER 7

ACCESS YOUR INTUITION

When you sync your soul with the Universe—that is, when you sync your inner energy with your outer energy—the magic of life truly starts to awaken.

CONNECTING YOUR SOUL AND THE UNIVERSE

Now that you know you are an energetic being living in an energetic Universe, you can see that what goes on inside of you is manifested outside of you and what manifests outside of you also manifests within you. One of the main bridges between your soul and the Universe is your intuition. Intuition is simply a strong feeling or sense of knowing. Your intuition is a Divine guiding force that can help you tap into both your soul and the Universe. This is because your intuition is receiving input from both of these sources.

REDISCOVERING YOUR INTUITION

To work effectively with the energy of the Universe, you have to trust and believe in your intuition and those gut feelings when they arrive. Intuition is a superpower we were all born with, but many of us have not learned or have forgotten how to use it. Your intuition is so powerful that it can guide you in life and support you when you are feeling at a crossroads. Using your intuition can also make you a more effective communicator and allow you to really understand the vibrational nature of the world around you.

We are all intuitive, but in order to really start listening and trusting our intuition, we have to develop it like a muscle. Just like the Universe is always speaking to you, so too is your intuition, and the quieter you can become the more you will be able to hear. Most of us have hundreds of thoughts that race through our mind every day.

In fact, most of us have so many thoughts that we may not even be able to tell what our intuition even sounds like. If you want to start strengthening your intuition and be able to hear it, you have to learn how to tame the thoughts of your mind. Your intuition speaks to you when your mind is still, so the first step to working with intuition, other than trusting yourself, is creating stillness.

FIRST, STILL YOUR MIND

Stilling your mind is really about bringing your awareness into the present moment and clearing all unnecessary chatter. The following activities will help you practice stilling your mind in easy, everyday ways. You might want to try them all, or just choose the one that speaks to you:

- Meditation is a classic way to still your mind. If you aren't sure how to start meditating, simply focus on your breathing, or just sit quietly and reflect.
- Journaling and creative activities like coloring, painting, or needlecrafts are great ways to silence your mind and bring your awareness into the present moment.
- Gardening and spending time in nature will force you to step away from electronic screens and look around.

Once you have found a way to still your mind, practice it on a daily basis: in the car, in the shower, early in the morning, or just before bed. Start making this part of your daily routine so you develop the habit. In fact, let us try it right now.

Exercise: Creating Stillness

Take five or six deep breaths in and out of your nose. As you breathe, focus on nothing except the rush of air moving in and out of your nose. Feel the coolness of the air, feel the expansiveness of your chest, feel the rising and falling of your belly. Focusing your awareness on the breath allows you to calm any racing thoughts or loud mental chatter so you can start tuning in to you.

When you start making stillness of the mind a regular practice, you will give your intuition more of a chance to show up and connect with you. You will also be opening the doorway to connecting with your own energy on a stronger and more powerful level.

OPENING YOUR THIRD EYE

Along with learning how to quiet the thoughts in your mind, the next most important step when working with your intuition is to open and activate your third eye. Your third eye is an energy center located in the middle of your forehead. When activated it can grant you access into your sixth sense, or intuition. Your third eye is also responsible for helping you raise your level of consciousness and strengthening the connection you have with the magic of the Universe. The third eye has also been connected to the pineal gland, a small endocrine gland in the vertebrate brain. The pineal gland has been revered by ancient cultures for centuries for its ability to connect us with the wisdom of the Universe and help us tap into higher realms of consciousness.

Opening the energy center of your third eye is going to help you open to your intuition and even Divine realms, which we'll learn more about later in this book.

A Third Eye in Your Wallet?

Symbolic images of the pineal gland and third eye can be seen on everything from ancient Egyptian hieroglyphics to Buddhist temples, Mesopotamian artifacts, and even on the US $1 bill.

THINGS THAT CAN BLOCK YOUR THIRD EYE

If you want to open your third eye, you need to take a mind-body approach. Mentally, you have to clear the clutter and create stillness. Physically, you have to nourish your body with clean, healthy food and avoid certain foods, chemicals, and substances that can block your third eye from opening.

The following practices can block your third eye:

- Consuming additives, preservatives, and artificial sweeteners
- Coming into contact with pesticides and toxic chemicals found in household cleaners
- Using drugs and alcohol
- Being exposed to electromagnetic radiation (sources include microwaves, Wi-Fi devices, cell phones, and the like)
- Eating a diet rich in meat
- Eating processed and refined foods
- Drinking carbonated, sugary beverages

- Drinking fluoridated water
- Applying cosmetics, perfumes, and body products that contain preservatives, fillers, and harmful chemicals

Of course, it's extremely difficult to eliminate all of these things from your life. But by limiting these influences as much as possible, you will have more success opening your third eye, and you will also improve your overall health and well-being.

THINGS THAT CAN OPEN YOUR THIRD EYE

It is also important to nourish your body with things that are going to help strengthen and open your third eye. These include:

- Eating a diet rich in organic fruits and vegetables
- Limiting your intake of animal products
- Eating superfoods like cacao, spirulina, goji berries, etc.
- Getting plenty of sunshine
- Sleeping an adequate amount every night
- Practicing meditation and positive thinking
- Eating raw foods
- Exercising regularly
- Using essential oils
- Using crystals
- Spending time in nature

As you can see, keeping your third eye open is very closely connected to living a healthy lifestyle. If you want to use your energy to tap into your intuition and higher realms, you have to first be able to take care of yourself and your life on earth.

Exercise: Activating Your Third Eye

Crystals are a powerful ally in your quest to open your third eye. This is because crystals have an extremely pure energetic frequency that can be used to stimulate healing and boost your own vibration. For this exercise, the recommended crystal to use is amethyst, as it carries a vibration that helps to unlock the intuition and offer protection. To do this exercise, you will need just two things: an amethyst crystal and some sunshine. In order to get the full benefit of the energy of the Sun, try to do this exercise when the Sun is either rising, setting, or at its highest point in the sky. Follow these steps:

1. Run your crystal under clean water for a few seconds.
2. Dry your crystal with a soft cloth and begin rubbing it between your hands in order to seal it with your energy.
3. Once the crystal feels charged up with energy and warm in your hands, place it on the center of your forehead, just above your eyes. Take a few deep breaths in and out. Visualize the purple energy of the amethyst going into your third eye and filling it up with activated energy.
4. Hold the amethyst in place, close your eyes, and look up toward the sunlight. (Please make sure your eyes are closed before looking at the Sun!) Gently take seven deep breaths in and out as you allow the sunlight to hit the crystal. Doing this once should be enough to begin activating the energy of your third eye; the rest of the work comes from practicing the use of your intuition as much as possible.

INTUITIVE FEELINGS

Now that you've learned how to access your intuition, what do you do when you hear it? For some of us, it might be a new and confusing sensation. When you receive an intuitive feeling, or what you think is an intuitive feeling, the first step is to trust it. By trusting your intuition and acknowledging it when it arises, you will strengthen its power. Following through on your intuitive hunches is also a great way to start experimenting with the accuracy of your intuition.

Your intuition is simply a strong feeling or knowing. Sometimes, however, your mind can get in the way and judge or put words on your intuitive feelings. Your fear kicks in and you immediately put a negative spin on what your intuition is trying to tell you. This judgment can sometimes be false, which can make you feel that your intuition cannot be trusted. For example, I once dated someone who I just had an uncomfortable feeling about. He was lovely, funny, and all the things that you would want your partner to be, but something just felt off about him. I brushed this feeling aside, but over time I began imagining all these horrible situations—he must be cheating on me, I thought, or lying to me; or maybe he is using me . . . Fear took hold as I began imagining the worst. Eventually, after torturing myself for too long, I decided to address this nagging feeling, and I confessed to him what I was feeling. It turned out that he was very religious and he knew that his family would never accept me because I was not the same religion. Even though my intuition was on to something, it was my fear that took over and allowed me to make up all of these terrible scenarios. In reality, this guy had done nothing wrong; he just couldn't commit due to the pressure of his family.

This example illustrates how your judgment can cloud your intuition. But this example also demonstrates that you can always trust your intuition; it is your mind that often gets in the way. This is why learning to still your mind is so important. To be a good receiver of your intuition, you have to resist judging and interpreting intuitive feelings when they arise.

IS IT INTUITION OR FEAR?

One of the most common hurdles when it comes to understanding your intuition is knowing whether it is actually your fears sending you the message instead of intuition. We are all intuitive, but when we ignore our intuition, usually fear steps in to take its place. When this happens, it can be very difficult to determine what is fear and what is intuition. In fact, when left untamed, fear can become the loudest voice in your mind.

It is no surprise that fear takes over, because we live in a society that is largely driven by fear: Fear of not being good enough, not being pretty enough, not having enough, and so on. In fact, there are so many fear-based messages out there that most of us carry around such fearful beliefs without even knowing it. When you begin to become aware of when you are operating with fearful thoughts, then you will be much more able to allow your intuitive voice to shine. If you have a strong feeling and you want to determine if it is indeed your intuition or just fear, here is how you can tell.

Your intuition:

- Feels like a strong sense of knowing and is not highly emotional
- Is heard instantly and is not repetitive

- Feels definitive, almost like there is no need to analyze or explain it
- Feels loving and supportive
- Is centered around the present moment

Your fear:

- Feels highly emotional and may even trigger feelings of anxiety or stress
- Activates your "flight or fight" response and creates a strong impulse or desire to take radical action that is highly emotional
- Is very repetitive and demanding and may require a lot more analysis
- Seems to have many variables and can create confusion or mixed feelings
- Feels very unsupportive or restrictive
- Is centered around the future or examples from the past

The most effective way to tell whether you are operating from your fear or your intuition is your emotional response. Because your intuitive voice is speaking with the wisdom and knowledge of your soul and the Universe, it is often very calming and straightforward.

Because fear can be a very powerful force, there are also situations where your intuitive voice initially sends you a message, but then your fear response kicks in and takes over. Although your intuitive message might be accurate, the amount of fear and dread surrounding the situation can make things feel very confusing and stressful. Your intuitive voice can also get lost in the thoughts of your mind, which makes its messages even harder to make sense of.

"Silence is the language of God, all else is poor translation."

—Rumi

To help you navigate through all of this, it is important to remember that your intuition is a strong sense of knowing. So if you feel this strong knowing, even if it is for just a moment, know that there is very likely some truth to it. If you are feeling overwhelmed about the message you have received, you may have to give yourself more time and space to fully process and accept what your intuition may be trying to show you or tell you. Just keep trusting the process and give yourself more time before following through. The more you can trust your intuition and not judge it, the easier it will be to work with it.

Exercise: Intuition Journal

Another way to strengthen your intuition is to start learning exactly how your intuition speaks to you. Everyone's intuition operates a little differently. Some people may feel tingles or butterflies in their stomach, others may receive visions or dreams, and others may hear messages. Your intuition may also speak to you using all of these mediums, but often, one method usually stands out as being the strongest. If you really want to develop your intuition and start seeing it in action, consider keeping an intuition journal. Whenever you have an intuitive thought or feeling, write it down in the journal. Be sure to note how and when the message arrived. This compilation will allow you to look back and reflect on your intuition and determine what it feels like and sounds like when it shows up in your life.

INTUITION IN ACTION

We have all experienced strong feelings that have guided us and provided us with insights about things that the logical mind just can't comprehend. One example of this comes from a friend of mine, a young actress who was in love with movies and the world of cinema. She would watch films for hours and write down the names of the directors and writers whom she wished to work with. One writer in particular stood out to her the most, and she wrote down in her journal that she just knew the two of them would work together one day.

Several years later, when she had forgotten all about this writer, she was at a costume fitting for a role she had booked. As she was having her fitting, she met some of the directors and crew as well as a man who introduced himself as the writer. To her surprise, it was the same writer who she had written about in her journal when she was younger. She couldn't believe that she got to work with him, but at the same time, she intuitively knew that one day she would. Their working relationship didn't just end there; in fact, the two of them still work together to this day and have created some amazing projects together. Somewhere deep down inside of her, her intuition just knew that she and this person would have a special connection.

Perhaps you see this in your own life when you meet someone for the first time. Intuitively you pick up on their energy and whether or not the person is someone who you want to develop a relationship with. We do this in romantic relationships especially, and within a matter of minutes on a first date often we know whether or not we want to keep seeing the person. This is an example of your intuition in action and when you start paying attention to it, it will start guiding you in a host of wonderful ways.

HOW YOUR INTUITION KNOWS THINGS THE MIND DOES NOT

As an intuitive reader, I use my intuition all the time to tune in to the energy that surrounds people. I can determine the quality of a person's energy and determine if there are any energetic blocks or stagnant emotions. I can also pick up on their feelings and perhaps the energy that is unfolding around them. Every intuitive reading is different and every person has a different energy that needs to be interpreted slightly differently, but one thing that is always the same is the way in which my intuition speaks to me. With practice, you too can tap into your own intuition and learn how to read the energy around yourself and others.

Tuning in to your intuition is really about tuning in to the voice of your soul. This voice can often understand things that the mind simply cannot. Intuition doesn't work based on logic. Instead, it is purely a feeling that seems to hold an unexplainable wisdom. This unexplainable wisdom comes from the knowing that lives inside all of us. Before an event can take place in reality, there has to be an energy buildup that causes the event to finally materialize in physical form.

When you tune in to the energy of the Universe and your own intuition, you can gain access to this buildup of energy and understand things before they happen. This is not about predicting the future; it is about understanding where your intuition gains its knowing from. Because your intuition also responds to energy, it can pick up vibes from other people, situations, and events. Your intuition may also be gaining knowledge from your past lives and from the life lessons that you were sent here to experience. All of this makes your intuition an extremely powerful source of information, as long as you know how to use it.

USING YOUR FEELINGS AS A GUIDE

To start working with your intuition on a more consistent basis, you have to get in touch with your feelings. This requires you to shift away from your mental thoughts and into a place of feeling. Getting in touch with your feelings requires you to move past any thoughts that are swimming around in your mind, and instead travel within to your heart center. In today's society, we are often out of touch with our feelings and gloss over them or even ignore them. It is not until we really sit in our own stillness and essence that we can understand how we are truly feeling.

Your feelings are a powerful compass for you in this life. When something makes you feel good, that is a clear sign from your intuition that you are on the right path and are heading in the right direction for you. When something feels off, uncomfortable, or wrong, that is also a sign from your intuition that you need to pay attention to what it is trying to tell you.

The Voice of Your Intuition

Your intuition often speaks to you as a whisper. You'll probably find that your true feelings are a lot gentler and more loving than you imagine. It is your mind that likes to twist things and create the fear and panic that you can sometimes feel.

If you are stuck about the direction of your life or about which path you should take, use your feelings to guide you. What feels the best to you in the present moment? When you ask yourself this question, stay in the present moment. Be mindful not to get stuck in the trap of thinking, "When I have this, then it will feel good" or "I will feel good when . . ." If you want to feel good in the future, you have to feel good in the now! The present moment is all you really have, so you have to focus your attention on the here and now. Again, this doesn't mean that you ignore planning or preparing for the future, but you have to center your ideas in the now.

For example, let's say you are deciding whether to quit your job or to stay. You are unhappy in your current position and have wanted to make some changes for a while. You are nervous about quitting, however, because you don't have another job lined up and aren't sure that you can financially support yourself while looking for another position. In this situation, you have to logically think about your future and ensure that your decision protects you in the long run; but at the same time, you can find the clues to the steps you need to take in how you really *feel* about the situation.

Still your mind and really ask yourself, "How do I feel about this situation?" When you silence your mind and listen to your feelings, you may be surprised at what is "behind" your dilemma. Often your feelings of frustration or angst come from your thoughts about the situation and not the situation itself. When you take away the thoughts and just center on that place of feeling, you may be able to uncover the emotions behind it all, such as your fears about quitting, or even a self-limiting belief about not being good enough to get the job you really want.

When you clear your mind and get to the root of how you feel, it may also illuminate the pathway forward. Even if no pathway seems to appear, simply acting on your true, deeper feelings may help you shift your awareness to something else. It is almost as if by washing away your thoughts, the heart can speak and your intuition can shine through.

When you follow what feels good to you, it is a pretty clear sign that you are heading in the right direction. As you take a step in a particular direction, notice how that step makes you feel. If you are scared, but excited, it is probably a good sign. But if the step forward just feels "off" in more ways than one, it could be a sign that there is a better option or path out there.

Exercise: Uncovering Your Feelings

If I asked you how you were feeling today, chances are you would reply with "great," "fine," or "okay." These are the most common words we use to describe how we feel. While one of those words may be an appropriate answer when meeting an acquaintance or talking to a cashier, they are not sufficient for deeper interactions. Unfortunately, these answers all too often become the norm even in our private lives. Take a minute now to really center yourself. Take a few deep breaths and then ask yourself the question, "How do I really feel?" Come up with three feeling words that describe how you are really feeling right now. You may surprise yourself by what emerges.

Focusing on your feelings rather than your thoughts, and allowing yourself to feel without judgment, provides a way for you to view things from an energetic perspective. Sometimes things seem to make sense when you view them from a place of logic, but it is more powerful to ask yourself how you really *feel* about the situation. When you really get in touch with your feelings, you start paving the way to understanding your intuitive voice. In fact, one of the most powerful ways to ask your intuition for guidance is by shifting away from your mental chatter and into a place of feeling.

HOW THE MOON CAN IMPACT YOUR FEELINGS

Your soul and the Universe are one, which means that whatever is happening in the Universe you also feel in your soul. The more empathetic you are, the more likely you are going to experience this phenomenon. Feelings are a powerful guide, but sometimes your feelings can also be amplified by the Universe. In fact, if you observe yourself carefully, you may see a parallel between what you are feeling and the cycles of the Moon.

We all know that the Moon has the ability to affect the tides, and seeing that we are also made up of mostly water, it is very likely that the Moon also has an effect on our bodies. The Moon has the ability to amplify whatever you are feeling. The specific way the Moon amplifies things depends on which phase or cycle it is in. On the night of a Full Moon, many people feel overly emotional; and on the night of the New Moon, many people feel withdrawn and introspective.

For centuries, people have looked to the Moon as a way of understanding their emotions and even their soul. When the Moon is at a peak in its cycle, it is able to amplify or illuminate things, allowing you to see and feel things with more certainty and clarity. This in turn can help bring to the surface any buried feelings or messages that you perhaps may not have been able to understand or fathom otherwise. By becoming aware of the cycles of the Moon, perhaps you may begin to notice how in sync you are with the energy of the Moon. One Moon cycle is 29.5 days, which is also about the same as a woman's menstrual cycle. The New Moon marks the start of a new cycle, the day when the seed is planted (or the lining of the uterus is shed); and the Full Moon marks the highest point of energy in the cycle, the day when the seed is in bloom (or when an egg is released in order to be fertilized). When you start paying attention to the different stages of the Moon, you may begin resonating with the energy of the cycle in your own life as well.

Exercise: Moon Journal

If you are curious how in sync you are with the cycles of the Moon, pay attention to any thoughts or feelings that come up for you for one complete Moon cycle. You can:

- Begin by writing down anything that you are feeling or experiencing around the time of the New Moon. The New Moon is a great time to think about starting new things, so perhaps write down or reflect on something that you would like to start or bring into your life.
- On the Full Moon, repeat this process by writing down anything you are feeling or experiencing. The Full Moon is typically a good time to release and let go, so notice if anything comes up for you around this time that you need to let go of and write it down.
- Repeat this process one more time on the next New Moon.

Once you have completed an entire Moon cycle, reflect back on what you wrote and see if you can observe any synergy between your life and the phases of the Moon.

HOW YOUR INTUITION SENDS MESSAGES

When you are unaware of your intuition, often it can try to send you signs or clues to remind you of its existence. This is especially true if your intuition is trying to convey a message to you. Just the same, if you ask for a sign or for an answer but are closed off from your intuition or are too focused on the outcome, then you might not detect the answer when it comes.

Your intuition can send you messages in many different ways, but some of the most common are:

1. A tingling sensation, chills, "butterflies," or goose bumps
2. A strong feeling of knowing
3. Prophetic dreams or vivid dreams that seem to carry a message
4. Hearing a song stuck in your head
5. A wave of inspiration while meditating, exercising, or showering
6. Feeling physically ill for no apparent reason, especially in the stomach or head
7. Feeling drawn to a particular person, activity, or destination
8. Thinking about someone and then seeing them or hearing from them

As you can see, there are so many ways that your intuition is able to deliver you messages and answers. The more in tune you get with yourself, the more open you will be to your intuition and how it chooses to communicate with you.

Exercise: Asking Your Intuition for Guidance

Use this exercise to practice and develop your intuition. Often all it takes for your intuition to become stronger is awareness and trust, so that's what this exercise focuses on. To ask your intuition for guidance, think of a question that you want your intuition to answer. Hold the question clearly in your mind and then ask yourself to think about everything that makes you fearful or scared surrounding this question. Write down the thoughts that come to you, along with any other pros and cons that your mind has conjured up for you.

Once you have allowed your mind to speak, it is time to listen to your intuition. Place your hand over your heart and then take three deep breaths, in and out. Bring your awareness to your breath and still your mind. Then, very gently, ask your heart the same question and give your intuition time and space to respond. Often the first whisper or the first feeling that you receive is the voice of your intuition.

When you start working with your intuition and the Universe, you might feel a very powerful shift in your life. Working with both of these energies allows you to see and experience the world from a completely different mindset. Difficult situations become clearer, your path becomes illuminated, and it is easier to see the miracles in everyday life. Working with your intuition takes constant practice, but in time it will soon become one of your driving superpowers. It will also help you to pay attention to your feelings, rather than the mental chatter of your mind.

THERE ARE NO WRONG PATHS

It is also important to remember that there are really no wrong paths in this life. The path you choose is always the perfect path for you, no matter how it may seem on the outside. At the end of the day, we are all here to grow and learn, and you chose the path that you chose for a specific reason. The reason could be that you needed to learn something or you needed to grow in some way in order to move forward in your life. All roads really do lead home, so if you are at a crossroads, or struggling to hear the voice of your intuition, take a single step and notice how that step makes you feel. Your feelings are always pointing you in the right direction, and you must be willing to go deep and actually feel them without your mind interfering.

ALL ROADS LEAD HOME

When I first got my driver's license (and this was before the widespread availability of GPS devices) I was super excited to be able to drive around town on my own. One day while out and about I got terribly lost trying to make my way home. I had a map in the car but I couldn't seem to make heads or tails of it. Eventually following the map resulted in me getting more lost and more mixed up.

I ditched the map and started aimlessly driving up and down and around, trying to find something that looked even remotely familiar.

I was starting to get extremely frustrated and anxious at this point, so I pulled over to the side of the road to regroup. In that moment I decided that the only thing I could do was get back on the road and follow my instincts. As soon as I felt compelled to turn, I would turn. As soon as I felt an instinct rise up, I would listen to it—for in that moment, that was all I had. Soon enough, I came across a familiar place! I was so happy and so relieved that in that moment of joy, a profound thought floated up from deep within my soul and into my consciousness: All roads lead home. The words hit me deeply, almost like they had been sent straight from my heart.

No matter how convoluted the path, no matter how lost you get on your journey, eventually you are going to wind up somewhere familiar and eventually you are going to find your way home to wherever you need to be.

CHAPTER WRAP-UP

Your intuition is like the bridge that connects the energy of your soul with the energy of the Universe. By tapping into your intuition, your are able to "download" information not only from your soul, but also the Universe as well. We all have an intuition, the trick is to simply trust it and use it frequently. Think of your intuition like a muscle, the more you flex it and use it, the stronger it is going to become. Your intuition is really like a superpower that can guide you through all of life's ups and downs, it is just up to you to make the most out of it.

- Opening your third eye energy center can help you activate your intuition and strengthen your intuitive abilities.

- Intuition speaks to everyone differently, but it often feels like a strong sense of knowing or understanding.
- Your intuition and your feelings often work in tandem. In fact, by tuning in to your true feelings, you can often begin to understand what your intuition is trying to tell you.
- Your feelings are also like a guidance system that can point you in the direction of your intuition and positive energy.
- In order to access your intuition, you have to first learn how to create stillness in your mind and clear the clutter of repetitive thinking.
- The cycles of the Moon can also influence your emotions and feelings, and can also intuitively guide you.

PART 3

Manifesting a Positive Life

CHAPTER 8

OVERCOME COMMON OBSTACLES

"Obstacles do not block the path; they are the path."

—Zen proverb

LETTING GO OF THINGS THAT NO LONGER SERVE YOU

As you become more aware of your energy and the energy of the Universe, you might find yourself getting stuck in repetitive patterns or running into the same problems again and again. Sometimes this type of obstacle appears when you are keeping certain behaviors, thought processes, or situations in your life that aren't in your best interest. When you keep things in your life that no longer serve you, it is often a sign that your mind, body, and soul are out of balance.

When you remove things from your life that no longer serve you—whether it's a job, relationship, or particular way of being—you allow yourself the opportunity to step into a realm of new possibilities. It allows you to enter into a void-like space where you really have the potential to create something new and exciting.

When you close a door in one area of your life, you enter a very creative phase. This is especially true when you close the door on a negative influence in your life. When you take action to remove something from your life from a place of love, the Universe will always guide and protect you. Almost as a "thank you" for looking after yourself, the Universe will grant you an amazing, supercharged potential to create and manifest what you want your next chapter to look like.

You do have some say in which door the Universe will open for you. Your say is determined through your thoughts, your energy, and the energy you are putting out into the world.

When you have released something from your life, the space that is now created is filled with the potential of infinite possibilities. When you make room for something new in your life, use the powerful creative energy around you to set your intention and send your wishes out into the

Universe. Remember, you have to feel and be the energy that you want to create. Set your intention, feel your intention, and then surrender to the outcome. When you align with your mind, body, and soul, you can naturally attract experiences that are perfect for you. When you get to the point in your life where you are clearing out things that no longer serve you, you are in the prime position to step up into your soul's fullest potential. This is because the only way to step into your true self is to shed everything that is weighing you down and blocking you from being you.

When One Door Closes, Another Always Opens

We live in an ever-providing Universe that is filled with opportunities. When you clear space in your life by ditching something that no longer serves you, the Universe always presents you with a new opportunity. This is helpful to keep in mind if something in your life ends abruptly, or when you are afraid of taking that leap of faith. As long as you can keep your energy open to receiving, the Universe is always going to grant you something new. Perhaps you have already been able to witness this in your own life. Have you ever let go of something, then had something better come along? Even if you liked the something that has gone, as the Dalai Lama once said, "Sometimes not getting what you want is a wonderful stroke of luck." The Universe works in mysterious ways and it may be impossible for you to always find the higher reason or cause, but that doesn't mean that one doesn't exist. It just means that it has not reached your level of consciousness just yet, and maybe it never will, and that is okay too. When one door closes, another door somewhere always opens. It is up to you to find it and walk through it.

Exercise: Getting Rid of Things That Don't Serve You

Start by making a list of all the things that are no longer serving you. These could be relationships, commitments, beliefs, habits, the way you treat yourself, and so on. Aim to get as many things as possible on your list—sometimes you have to dig a little bit in order to uncover all the things that no longer serve you. Once you have your list, see if you can find one or two things that really stand out to you. The biggest items on your list might actually be responsible for many other problematic things in your life—and perhaps you never even realized it. For example, if your job is no longer serving you, its influence could be spilling over into other areas of your life and contributing to other things that are no longer serving you like a negative attitude, poor relationships with your family, or even self-deprecating thoughts.

When you keep negative people, jobs, or commitments in your life, they have a ripple effect and start to make other areas of your life negative as well. But sometimes the process of fixing, clearing, or shifting a few things that are no longer serving you can have profound effects in your life.

Now it is time to think of solutions. Forget all the problems, fears, and baggage that come along with these areas and keep your energy focused on the solution. Ask yourself: "Is there anything I can do that can allow me to change this situation into one that serves me?" "Can I shift my mindset?" "Can I try a new strategy?" "Can I communicate my feelings better?" If the situation can't be changed for the better by your efforts, then you may have to consider dumping it from your life.

LEARN HOW TO SURRENDER

One of the most powerful things you can do in your life is to surrender to the things that are not in your control. In this life you can only be responsible for yourself, your actions, and your thoughts. Everything else is somewhat beyond your control. When you surrender to this and accept the things you cannot control, it makes life less stressful and it allows you to embrace the flow of the Universe. When you surrender to who you are, to your life, and to the Universe, that is when you can truly be guided.

LEARNING TO LET GO

If you want to experience what your soul truly came here to do in this magical Universe, you need to learn how to release and let go. Many of us understandably have a hard time surrendering. We carry around old pains and thoughts for years, holding on to them out of fear or because that is all that we have known.

> *"God grant me the serenity to accept the things I cannot change, the courage to change the things I can, and the wisdom to know the difference."*
>
> —Reinhold Niebuhr

If you hold on to the past, or cling to expectations of the future, it can be very difficult for you to create a meaningful life that feels in sync with the Universe. When you are so caught up in everything, it blinds you and makes you feel confused, afraid, or even anxious. So many of us fall into the trap of holding on to the pains, regrets, and sorrows of the past. So many of us fall into the trap of telling the same story over and over again. Just the same, so many of us worry about the future and attempt to plot and plan every step of our lives. We all know that life doesn't go according to plan, but many of us still get disappointed or upset when our expectations are not met.

Exercise: Releasing the Past

To be able to surrender to the flow of your life, you have to first learn how to surrender and release the past. To find out what you should surrender, ask yourself these questions: "What emotions, thoughts, or events am I still churning over again and again in my mind?" "Is there an old story that I keep telling myself?" Write down your answers on a piece of paper. Keep writing until all your thoughts and feelings surrounding the situation have been shared. When you feel ready, take a deep breath and on your exhale, start ripping the paper. As you exhale, you can also visualize yourself releasing all the emotions and attachments to your story. Keep doing this till the entire paper is in shreds.

Surrendering and letting go allows you to release any expectations or painful past memories and frees you to embrace and accept whatever comes your way. When you don't have expectations or judgments about your life and who you are, you give yourself more room to accept what does flow into your life. This allows you to feel at peace with whatever situations come your way and keeps you from being thrown off track or anxious.

Recall the metaphor of the blooming flower we imagined in Chapter 1. Having expectations for the future would be similar to trying to dictate what a flower is going to look like before it has bloomed. Until the flower has blossomed, however, there is no telling exactly what it may look like. Remember, your soul is the seed of that flower. As long as you are nourishing the seed and looking after it, the rest will take care of itself. You don't have to force the flower to bloom or micromanage the flower's ability to bloom, or feel anxious about the flower. You just do what you can, let go, and trust that the flower is going to bloom into whatever it needs to be . . . at its own pace and in its own time.

FREEING YOURSELF FROM THE PAST

Holding on to the past makes it very difficult for the Universe to send you anything new.

Releasing Doesn't Mean Forgetting

Releasing the past is not about forgetting the past. It is about loosening your attachment to the thoughts and feelings that the past events have stirred. We all have both fond and haunting memories, but the less attached you become to them, the easier it will be for you to move forward.

If you stay caught in the past, you may find that you begin playing out the same events in your life over and over again. You may enter into new relationships with similar people, or the same theme may present itself in your life again and again. You also may find it difficult to move forward, or you might feel blocked and restricted when you do try to make a move. To release the past, you have to truly want to let go of your attachment to those events.

Sometimes we like to hold on to painful memories or situations because it helps us justify our status as victims and gives us a reason for not being able to achieve what we want in life. But this mindset just creates a never-ending cycle. Retelling a story again and again about how you were hurt and how you were wronged is never going to bring healing and closure. Instead, it keeps the past alive in your mind and alive in your body. This creates more pain and more agony—and it doesn't serve anyone, least of all you.

When life doesn't go the way you expected, or you find yourself in circumstances that are undesirable, it can be very tempting to enter into victim mode. You might ask yourself, "Why me?" This victim mode then leads to blaming yourself and others, which then leads to shame. This vicious cycle ultimately leaves you feeling sorry for yourself. You may also push your victimhood onto others, and feed off other people's sympathy and attention. But this sympathy and attention will only last so long before people get tired of hearing the same story over and over again. This is a pattern that we all get stuck in at times, but take heart: You can consciously break the cycle.

BREAKING THE VICTIM CYCLE

Breaking the "poor me" victim cycle starts by becoming aware of it. Once you are aware that you are doing it, it becomes easier for you to stop yourself from going to that place. Whenever you feel that type of negative energy, stop yourself and then gently shift your attention elsewhere. Try everything you can to stop yourself from saying the same things and engaging in the same habits. Your goal is to stop the same pattern from playing out in your mind. Journaling is a great way to help break the cycle, as it allows you to get your thoughts and feelings down on paper.

In order to release attachments to the past, you have to confront the past and confront what is making you hold on to the story. When you can allow yourself to feel what you need to feel, often the emotion dissipates. It is denying yourself the feelings, or denying the events of the past, that cause you to hold on and never want to let go.

Often we hold on to pain because it is too painful to process. It seems counterintuitive, but so many of us are afraid to fully feel the pain and the hurt, so it stays around like a gentle hum, reminding us of its presence every single day. Living this way can whack you out of alignment and make it difficult for you to open to and receive the Universe.

Exercise: Be Here

Take a moment to ask yourself: What do you want your "here" moment to look like? What do you want your "here" moment to feel like? You have the power, you have the control to feel how you want to feel in this very moment, and you have the power and the control to dictate what you are going to make of this moment. Are you going to live another moment stuck in the pains of the past? Or are you going to free yourself by surrendering to the present moment and accepting whatever this moment brings?

After you process the emotions, leave the past in the past and turn your awareness onto the present moment. Sometimes we can become so caught up in the painful memories of the past that our emotions color what really happened, or what really unfolded. The truth only exists in the present moment; everything else is just a memory that is forever connected to your thoughts and feelings about the event. To really release the past, you have to allow yourself to feel any painful emotions and then simply accept them and the situation for what it is. The past is gone. You are here now, and to live peacefully you have to align with being "here." Once you center your energy in this way, you automatically allow yourself to start thinking about ways that you can move forward with your life.

ACCEPT WHATEVER LIFE BRINGS YOU

To feel at peace, you have to first accept yourself—accept your perceived gifts, talents, flaws, shortcomings, mistakes, and let go of any unfair expectations you have placed on yourself. You also have to accept your life and the situations that unfold and embrace them wholeheartedly. You have to accept everything about yourself and your life. In fact, you must accept it so much that it is like you chose everything that has unfolded before you. When you bring this level of authentic acceptance into your life, it allows you to:

- Truly embrace all that you are.
- Continue shedding the self-limiting beliefs that hold you back.
- Surrender and relax.
- Step into a place of action.
- Shift your focus away from the problem and onto the solution.
- Remove any stress about the event or situation.
- Think outside the box and consider a bigger picture vision.

Life is always going to keep unfolding around you, and you can either allow it to strangle you and swallow you up or you can join the rhythm and flow of it and embrace it for all that it is. The choice is up to you. At any given moment you have the choice to believe that everything that is sent your way is either a blessing or a curse, there is no right or wrong, but which one would you rather move through life believing?

Self-Acceptance Is Self-Love

Acceptance is an act of self-love, and it can sometimes be the most powerful thing we can give ourselves. Sometimes just the smallest act of self-acceptance can be exactly what we need to move forward. Even just repeating the affirmation *"I love and accept myself"* to yourself can have profound benefits.

THE WEIGHT IS LIFTED

When you first start digging deep and releasing stuck emotions, it can leave you with a truly profound feeling of healing and release. In fact, it can be liberating, almost like you can finally shrug off the heavy coat that you have been carrying around. This feeling can be so euphoric that clearing out old and stagnant emotions can become a top priority. Many people who start clearing out old emotional baggage actually get addicted to the process and feel the need to dig up every last painful memory and childhood experience.

While this process can be extremely powerful and healing, eventually you also need to reach a point where you decide to make peace with exactly who you are. I actually don't think it is ever really possible to understand yourself on the deepest of levels. This is not only because we are always changing and evolving, but also because there are certain depths of our subconscious mind and our soul that we may never truly understand. Perhaps this is okay. Perhaps this is the way it was meant to be. To understand every nuance and to dissect every thought would take more than a lifetime, so eventually we have to stop digging and just start living.

We all have pains, we all have hurts, we all have traumas. Sometimes you have to just accept where you are and start loving yourself for exactly who you are, flaws, pains, and all. This is not about burying your pains or hurts, rather it is about accepting and loving them wholeheartedly without the need to analyze every single one of them. You will know when you have reached this point on your healing journey when you feel the call to move forward and take action in your life. You may not have all the pieces worked out or in place, but if you feel the flow of life inspiring you to take action, simply accepting and loving your past and all the baggage may be enough to give you the push forward that you need.

REMOVING THE MASKS YOU HIDE BEHIND

One of the hardest things about accepting yourself is the fear of what other people will think of you. When you shed the mask that you are wearing, you allow people to see you for exactly who you are. Yet when you embrace who you are, it also causes inauthentic people and situations to slip away from your life, leaving you with those who love you for you.

When you accept yourself, it is also very difficult to hide your true thoughts or how you really feel. This place of vulnerability can be terrifying, and therefore it is a lot easier for you to move through life with your mask securely fastened. Most of us actually have a cupboard full of masks that we wear in order to adapt to different social situations. While having these masks is somewhat necessary in this world, when you find yourself wearing a mask all the time, or with your close friends, partner, family, and so on, you can block yourself off from the authenticity of your soul.

When you fight to accept yourself you may also create inauthentic relationships that constantly feel like an effort or struggle to maintain. In fact, if you are in a particular relationship that constantly feels like a struggle, it may be because you have not shared your true authentic self with the other person or vice versa.

Many of us get so comfortable wearing our masks that we forget who we really are underneath it all. This causes us to become the people we think we need to be, rather than the people we truly are. Living your life this way can shift you out of alignment and make it very difficult for you to truly feel at peace with your life.

Being authentic is not about trying to be a mystical "better" version of yourself who has life all figured out neatly. Forget all of that. Embrace yourself for who you are right now, no matter how perfect or imperfect you feel yourself to be. Accept yourself and be truthful to who you are. When you do that, some relationships may slip away, but what you will be left with is a far more authentic and real life.

DEALING WITH CONFLICT AUTHENTICALLY

When you start acting from a place of authenticity and acknowledging your true thoughts and feelings, you can sometimes cause shifts not just in your life, but in the lives of those around you. No longer will you tolerate relationships that are inauthentic or that no longer serve you. No longer will you tolerate people who cross your boundaries or have little respect for you. No longer will you tolerate feeling like you have to wear a mask and pretending to be someone you are not.

When you have been operating your life through fear and doubt for a long time, it can actually be hard for you to see whether the friendships, relationships, or career path you have are fulfilling the authentic you or just the mythical version of you. When you drop the mask and start accepting yourself wholeheartedly, the things that are no longer in vibrational alignment with who you truly are begin to slip away.

This shift may require you to address some of these situations head-on. For example, if your boss has constantly undermined your efforts or made you feel miserable, tolerating this without a mask no longer becomes easy to do. Instead, the only way around it is to confront the situation. Many people, understandably, have a fear of confrontation and standing up for themselves. No one likes to be confronted or "told off," which is why we tend to shy away from doing it to others. It is a lot easier to go on pretending like things don't bother you than it is to speak up and share your immediate truth. When you bottle up your feelings, however, the inner conflict within you starts to grow, and you end up feeling frustrated, angry, and resentful toward that person. This creates a negative relationship and eats away at you on the inside.

THE CALM APPROACH

While it is not always necessary to express *every* thought and feeling, sometimes it is necessary to express your truth and stand up to people who have hurt you. Many people mistakenly believe that conflict has to be aggressive. It doesn't. Conflict can be approached in a constructive and calm way. In fact, approaching potential conflicts with a calmness and casualness can help to take the stress out of things. When having these conversations, it is always best to stick to "I" statements (for example: "I don't feel good when you . . ."). Such "I" statements allow you to take responsibility for the situation and ownership of your feelings. When you take ownership of your feelings, you also stop the other person from automatically going into a defensive mode. You can't really be annoyed at someone for how they feel, so by owning your feelings and using "I" statements, you encourage the other person to listen rather than to feel attacked by what you are saying.

FOCUS ON YOUR OWN JOURNEY

You can't please everyone and you can't compromise for everyone. You are going to come across people in life who don't respect you or who don't show mutual courtesy, and this is okay. In fact, how others react is not really even your business nor do such reactions have anything to do with you. You may be affected by them, but the truth is that you have no idea what inner demons or what thoughts and feelings other people may be struggling with. In this way, it is not fair to judge or make assumptions about a person based on their behavior. You don't have to tolerate the behavior, but at the same time you also need to understand that everyone is on their own journey.

We are all just visitors to this earth and we are all here to learn from each other and enjoy each other. This life is just a temporary moment in time that is part of a much bigger picture. We have all come from the same place and we will all return to the same place, so love others to the best of your ability but more importantly, love yourself so much that you can't help but act with authenticity.

EVERYONE IS A TEACHER

The people you meet in life who you have the strongest resistance to are often your greatest teachers. While everyone is a teacher, certain people in your life are going to deliver your most profound lessons. Sometimes the lessons are in learning how to say no or how to create boundaries to bad behavior or in learning how to push yourself to try new things.

A NEW KIND OF SOULMATE

Often, we are drawn to people who we intuitively know are going to be able to teach us and help us to grow. In fact, people who walk into your life and shake things up in a dramatic way are often soulmates who have been sent to help awaken your soul and remind you of why you are here and what you need to be doing. Many people think of soulmates only on a romantic level, but really a soulmate is anyone who comes into your life to help awaken you on some level so you can shift and change your life. This means that a soulmate even can be your pesky boss who drives you to change jobs or your annoying sister who seems to push every single one of your buttons. If you can open your awareness to look at these teachers in this way, you will be much more open to receiving their messages.

LEARNING TO LOVE EVERYONE

It is important to remember that everyone is on their own journey and that everyone is doing the best they can based on their level of consciousness. No one wants to be a "bad" person; no one wants to commit terrible acts or cause pain. Some people become this way because they are in pain and they have forgotten who they truly are. These people need love, not judgment. These people need light and not more of the same darkness they receive from the rest of the world.

Exercise: Sending Love to Others

Sending love to your loved ones is easy, but sending love to someone who has wronged you or who you want out of your life is much more difficult. Yet sending love is a good way to move forward and to cleanse away any lingering energy from old lovers or friends. To do this, simply imagine the person in your mind's eye and then repeat aloud or to yourself, *"I send you light and loving energy, but I now release you from my life. It is time to go."* You can keep repeating this statement a few times till you feel your intention is cemented.

Loving everyone does not mean you should tolerate bad behavior or put yourself in a position where you know you are going to get hurt; rather, it is about simply accepting and acknowledging everyone who comes into your life without judgment. Just because you love someone doesn't mean you need to trust them or keep them as friends. When you love and accept people for who they are, you actually allow yourself to stop giving that person your time and energy. When you wallow in what someone else has done, or in someone else's behavior, you keep that energy alive inside of you. That, in turn, makes it very difficult for you to move on and feel at peace. By simply sending your love, you also allow yourself to move on with your life in a healthier way.

HOW TO FIND FORGIVENESS

We all have people in our lives who have disappointed us or who have let us down; people who have taken something from us or have left us feeling withered and broken. These people may have lied, cheated, hurt, abused, and caused a great deal of pain. These people may have caused you so much hurt that there is no possible way you could ever imagine forgiving them, let alone sending them loving energy. Often these situations haunt you for the rest of your life . . . unless you can find forgiveness inside of yourself.

> *"You practice forgiveness for two reasons: to let others know that you no longer wish to be in a state of hostility with them and to free yourself from the self-defeating energy of resentment. Send love in some form to those you feel have wronged you and notice how much better you feel."*
>
> —Wayne Dyer

It's time to look at forgiveness in a whole new light. Forgiveness is not about saying that what the person did was right, nor is forgiveness about condoning someone's bad behavior. Forgiveness is about accepting events in a way that allows you to send love and healing to the person and the event so that you can move on. Let's say a good friend lied to you. Obviously this would be painful because you considered the person to be someone you trusted and respected. Whether you choose to stay friends with this person or not is your choice, but either way you need to heal from the hurt. And the only way you can heal is through forgiveness. Even though you are not condoning the act, forgiving your friend is about accepting what happened in a way that allows you to let go of any pain or anger and move on without holding a grudge.

Exercise: How to Forgive Yourself

Forgiving yourself is one of the most powerful things you can do. Guilt and shame will never serve you, so give permission to let them go and forgive yourself. Here is how: Place your hand over your heart, close your eyes, and take two to three deep breaths in and out. Repeat softly to yourself, "I forgive you." Keep repeating this statement twenty one times with feeling. Notice how easy or difficult it is to say this to yourself. If tears or other emotions come up for you, don't block them, just let them flow. Once done, wrap your arms around your shoulders like you are giving yourself a big, warm hug.

This exercise is powerful enough, but if you want to dig a little deeper begin journaling any emotions, thoughts, or feelings that came up for you while doing the exercise. Repeat this exercise daily for at least a week for maximum benefits.

When you can find it in your heart to forgive, it also will be a lot easier for you to let go of the situation and to break any negative attachments to those involved. Finding forgiveness may be difficult at first, but if you simply open up some space to even consider forgiveness, then you've made a positive step. You may be surprised at just how healing even that small step can be. Perhaps consider for a moment how you may feel if you forgave yourself and others for all the things that you have been holding on to. Forgiveness is mostly about bringing you peace, because without forgiveness you may have great difficulty moving on and creating a life that allows you to trust others and yourself.

HOLDING ON TO GUILT

A friend of mine was having a rough breakup with her boyfriend. I was friends with both of them, so I often felt as if I was caught in the middle of their arguments. Their fighting got so bad at one point that each of them would call me to vent. Eventually I grew tired of being the middleman and felt it necessary to set some boundaries. One day my friend called me and wanted to stay over for the night. She had a terrible fight with her boyfriend and didn't want to go back to their shared place. In the moment when she asked me, I felt so tired and fed up with their antics that I told her no. I told her that she really needed to face up to whatever issues she was having and sort them out once and for all. She accepted the answer, but actually ended up staying at another friend's house for the night.

After saying no to my friend and finding out she went elsewhere, waves of guilt started flooding in. How could I have done that to her? How could I have turned her away when she was in need? I put myself in her shoes and knew that if I was in her position I too would have wanted to count on my friend to be there for me when I needed her. These thoughts continued to build and build until they began eating away at me. It didn't matter that my friend had accepted my no; deep down on the inside I was beating myself up for it every single day. Eventually time passed and the guilt was pushed away and forgotten.

It wasn't until years later that I realized this guilt had really affected our friendship. The effects weren't immediate or even noticeable, but the guilt had caused a shift in the friendship. Because I felt so guilty, I started overcompensating in the friendship and began giving away a lot of my time and energy in order to make up for it. This eventually changed the friendship and made it very difficult to maintain.

When one individual is holding on to guilt or uncomfortable emotions that are not expressed, on some level the growth and development of the relationship is thwarted. Even though the events were long gone and forgotten, the energy of it stayed alive within me and ended up being a contributing factor to the gradual falling apart of our friendship. In fact, it wasn't until this friendship fell apart that I realized just how much guilt I was carrying around about that one event, and how it had made me feel about the friendship. Once I was able to identify the guilt it created space for me to start forgiving myself. There are many ways to practice forgiveness, but in this situation I simply accepted the guilt and repeated to myself "I forgive you." Instantly, this allowed me to feel at peace.

This is a small example, but it allows you to see just how holding on to these emotions and not forgiving yourself or others can really damage the trust that you feel in your relationships and with life at large. No matter what you have done, no matter how you have hurt someone or betrayed someone or even seemingly ruined their life, there is always room to forgive yourself. You are always worthy of forgiveness, and when you can find it in your heart to forgive, waves of peace that you so very much deserve will follow.

The Guilt of Losing a Loved One

I once had a client who lost her baby at a very young age. The baby was born with a brain complication that the doctors didn't recognize until it was too late. Even though years had passed since her baby's death, she was still holding on to a lot of guilt. She felt as a mother that she should have known that something was wrong, and that she should have done something about it sooner. She had played over every scenario in her mind, beating herself up for all these things that she could have or should have done. She knew that these thoughts weren't helping her, but she had become stuck and her guilt had started eating away into all areas of her life. She so badly wanted to have another child but she was also terrified that the same thing would happen.

As we were going through the session I suddenly felt a little tap on my shoulder and a rush of energy. I couldn't see him, but I knew her son was now in the room with us. I have had some encounters with spirits before, but this was the first time a spirit had come through so clearly. I was unsure about what to do, but I decided that I just had to roll with it and so I began relaying the information her son was telling me. Needless to say, my client was extremely overwhelmed but also very excited by what was happening. All the while, I was feeling an immense love pouring in from her son that was so incredible it felt strong enough to heal all the wounds of the world! The love coming in from this spirit was so beautiful and healing that even I was deeply touched and moved by the entire experience.

I am not a medium and I do not offer this as a service, but on this day it just so happened that this is what needed to occur. This little boy came through because he needed to deliver a message to his mother. He needed to tell her that he was more than fine, that she did nothing wrong, and that he loved her unconditionally and wholly. This is one of those experiences you never forget, and it serves as a strong reminder that when you love yourself and allow love to flood your being, there is no reason to hold on to guilt or pain.

MAINTAINING A POSITIVE STATE OF BEING

We all know what positive energy feels like, but how can we maintain this positive state of being? When you remember who you are at your core—universal love—you will find that it is impossible for you not to feel some sense of joy radiating through. Still, life can bring you challenges that make it very difficult for you to feel positive. These events can wear you down and cause your vibration to grow dim. This is a normal and natural part of life and your soul's journey. You were meant to experience a whole spectrum of energy and a whole spectrum of vibrations. It is only when you experience the duality of the Universe that you can understand it. For light there has to be darkness; for happiness there has to be sorrow.

Only when you can see things as a whole, rather than just focusing on one aspect, can you truly stay in alignment. Even in your darkest hours, if you can remind yourself that you are a being of energy and that this feeling is temporary, you will see the love of the Universe staring back at you. This is part of the process of living life in a fuller and richer way.

Think of life like playing a video game. When you first start playing the game, you learn the basics. You learn how to move your avatar around the virtual world and you learn which buttons to press and click, and at what time. If this is where you stopped, if you never looked at any of the other features or advanced functions of the video game, you would never fully be able to enjoy it to the fullest of its capacity. Eventually, you may even reach a point in the game where you feel limited, stuck, or unable to move on. Maybe you would even reach a point in the game where you would start feeling negative or like a failure.

Life is very similar to this. Most of us stop learning how to live our lives beyond what we see. This causes our mindset to become extremely limited, narrow, and focused. We forget that we have other features, special tools, and functions that we can learn how to operate. We forget that life is meant to be a journey of constant learning. We forget that for every problem we have, there is also a solution, and that we just have to learn a new function or rule of the game in order to access it. When you find yourself feeling stuck in negativity or stuck in your life, often it is because you have outgrown your knowledge of the game. When you reach this place, you need to learn more tools and steps in order to find a solution and move forward.

There is a whole big world out there for you to see, and there is an infinite variety of tools and special features that are always manifesting in your life. But if you are closed off to them, no matter how hard you try, you are never going to see them. If your life were a video game, what would you do differently? Would you not want to explore every aspect of your game? Would you not want to learn all the features and tools so you can win or find secret levels? Life may not come with a set of tools and steps that everyone can follow, but your soul surely does come with an inner wisdom that will guide you.

There is no generic guidebook to life, but within us all is every answer to every question we could possibly ever ask. To enjoy this knowledge base, you have to start broadening the way you experience your life. You have to start seeing life and all the solutions that it has to offer. Your life is a video game with so many special features, shortcuts, prizes, tools, and buttons that you probably don't even have time to explore them all. But the more you can open yourself, the more you can open your mind to different ways of living your life, the easier it is going to be for you to see problems as challenges that can always be solved.

WHAT TO DO WHEN YOU FEEL STUCK

You have followed all the rules, done all your homework, and have started thinking positively. You hit the occasional bump, but you keep moving forward. But then you hit another bump and another, and then all of a sudden you are stuck. Perhaps you feel like all the positive thoughts in the world are not enough to lift you out of this valley. You may even feel that you don't need positivity; you need answers and fast.

When you reach a point in your life where you feel stuck, often it is because there is more information that needs to be processed where you currently stand. Feeling stuck is almost like the Universe's way of saying *Stop! Slow down and pay attention.* Until something shifts, or you realize whatever it is that you need to realize, you are going to remain where you are. It is only when something shifts or when your energy shifts that you can pull yourself out of a stuck situation.

Understanding this concept is relatively easy, but actually putting it into practice is more difficult. Often, you know that change needs to happen to get yourself unstuck, but you don't know what *kind* of change. To unstick yourself, you first have to raise your thought process to a place that you want to be at, like a place of clarity or knowing, and then tackle the issue from that state of consciousness. You cannot solve your problems from the same consciousness that created them. To get to this higher place, you need to take your focus off the situation and put it onto something else. Think of it like you are taking a pause from the problem so you can regroup your thoughts and energy. Try to relax during this pause, and try not to focus on the energy or situation that is causing you to feel stuck. Switch your thinking entirely and start focusing on what you feel certain about, rather than what you feel confused about or stuck with. This sense of security will instantly start to raise your vibration and get you aligned into a pattern that is aimed at helping you to think clearly.

After a few days of a pause, return to the difficult situation and see if you can think of a fresh new solution. Remember that you are never really stuck. The world keeps on moving and things keep on flowing—what gets stuck is your energy and your thinking.

So, whenever you are feeling stuck and no amount of positive thinking can shift your state, take a break, a pause, and focus on things that make you feel good. In due time you will be able to come back to your issue with a newfound perspective.

CHAPTER WRAP-UP

Life is always going to be presenting you with challenges, but this is how you grow. If you always had everything figured out in life there would be no fun and no mystery. You don't need to have everything perfect and smooth in order to live a positive life, you just need to embrace every obstacle and challenge as part of the journey. Think of your life like a video game—the challenges keep it interesting, force you out of your comfort zone, and help you to grow. We all signed up for this in some way or another, so why not choose to enjoy it and find the fun as you go along?

- Obstacles are not blocks in your path, rather they are part of your path and part of the journey.
- When you clear things from your life that are no longer serving you, it allows you the freedom to fill your life with something new and exciting.
- When you start acting from your true and authentic self you allow yourself to not only accept yourself but also accept and see the best in others.
- Everyone that comes into your life is a powerful teacher who is there to help you grow.
- Learning how to forgive is a powerful tool that can help you always feel free and in the vibration of positive and loving energy.
- It is normal to feel stuck or held back on your journey at certain times. When this feeling arises, use it as a time to reflect and pause. Try to focus on your thoughts and see if you can identify any repetitive stories or thought patterns that need to be released.

CHAPTER 9

EMBRACE HIGHER REALMS

The entire Universe is working in your favor. Everything in life is unfolding for your highest good, and when you can start to surrender and trust in the Divine plan you open yourself up to a whole new realm of being.

WHAT IS YOUR HIGHER SELF?

When you align with who you are, trust your intuition, and start paying attention to the signs and signals of the Universe, your entire life starts to shift to a new level. This place of being is commonly referred to as your Higher Self. When you operate your life as your Higher Self, things align almost as if by magic. Synchronicities appear, the right doors open at the right time, and you feel a sense of protection as you move through the Universe. When you operate from your Higher Self, you understand intrinsically that life is simply an experience that is supposed to help you grow and evolve.

When you operate from your Higher Self, you can:

- View problems that arise as opportunities of self-discovery.
- See the bigger picture of your life and understand how you fit into it.
- Rise above petty dramas and common complaints and step into a place that is more expansive and solution-minded.
- Understand the lessons and experiences that are sent your way.
- Operate from a place of non-attachment. (This means that instead of being attached to ideas, outcomes, and your physical identity, you are able to view life as a more fluid experience.)
- Use your feelings as the primary guiding force for how you move through life.
- Follow your intuition because you hear it strongly.
- See things from a more positive and optimistic viewpoint.
- Realize that everyone who has come into your life is part of your lesson and part of the bigger picture.
- Acknowledge that your thoughts play a powerful role in shaping your reality.

It is almost like all the seriousness and stress that life once contained melts away, and you are able to just trust, enjoy, and go with the flow. You understand at your core that through surrendering, and simply following your intuition and the signs of the Universe, the pieces of your life will naturally fall into place. Operating from your Higher Self allows you to feel that whatever is supposed to come your way will, and that whatever needs to go will go.

YOUR HIGHER SELF SHOWS YOU THE HIGHEST PATH

Most of us access our Higher Self at different moments throughout the day, perhaps without even realizing it. Accessing your Higher Self does not mean visiting some mythical place of enlightenment that only a select few gurus can reach. Everyone can operate from this place as long as they have the awareness to do so. Being at your Higher Self is really about functioning at the most optimal level for you. It means that you are reaching your fullest potential in this life and living up to who you truly are.

If you ever feel the calling to do something bigger with your life, if you ever feel the calling that there is something else out there for you, then this is likely your Higher Self calling to you. This is the calling of your soul. In order to answer, you have to start thinking bigger and shifting your mindset away from fears and self-limiting beliefs and into a more expansive and self-loving place.

There are many paths for you to take in this life, but your Higher Self is able to walk the "highest path." This is the path that allows you to reach your fullest potential. On this highest path you tap into those callings to do something bigger or to make more of an impact, and it allows your soul to achieve all it was sent to achieve.

Train to Be the Best

Let's be clear: There are no wrong paths. But when you are walking your highest path, your soul is performing at its fullest potential. Think of an athlete. If an athlete trains, eats the right food, and gets plenty of rest, the athlete is going to be able to perform at her best. However, if the athlete abandons her training she will not be able to perform at her peak. Walking your highest path is very similar to this. When you are operating at your peak, the experiences that come into your life are peak experiences, and they help stretch you to your ultimate potential. When you hide your potential or fail to step up to the plate and commit to your life, the path that you start to walk only allows you to live up to part of your potential.

Your highest path is, of course, not a literal path; it is really a state of being. To put it simply, when you are operating from your most optimum place, your life reflects that. When you are hiding in the shadows and failing to step up to who you really are, your life also reflects that.

ASKING FOR DIVINE HELP

We all have times in our lives when no amount of analyzing, letting go, or sitting in stillness is going to help tame the emotions we may be feeling. We all have times in our lives when no matter how hard we try to be centered, no matter how much we trust in the Universe to help us find our highest path, we feel overwhelmed and betrayed. This is normal and natural; however, this state of being is also temporary. Eventually, even in the pit of your darkest night, the light will shine through.

When you are in this dark place, there is a resource you can tune in to. While the Universe is always on your side, sometimes it helps to call on something more specific. Sometimes it helps to call on someone who was assigned to help you navigate through this life. Perhaps you are not aware that when you came into this life you were given a team of helpers. This team was sent to help guide you through your challenges and triumphs, and offer you guidance and support whenever you need a shoulder to lean on. This team of helpers is your Spirit Team, and we all have one.

WHAT IS YOUR SPIRIT TEAM?

Your Spirit Team is made up of your Higher Self and your soul, your intuition, your Spirit Guides, and Guardian Angels. These beings operate at a higher level of consciousness and were assigned to help you navigate through the world. Even though we all have a Spirit Team, many of us don't even realize it exists. Often a crisis of some kind can reveal our Spirit Team to us, but you don't have to wait for a crisis to connect. Simply trusting in them and asking them to come through can also be enough.

Even if you have not encountered Angels or Spirit Guides on your journey so far, sometimes just believing in a higher power can be enough for you to start seeing signs or experiencing feelings that are supported by your Spirit Team.

Your Intuition Is on Your Spirit Team

Your Spirit Team also includes your Higher Self and your soul, which speaks to you through your intuition. If you have ever had an intuitive feeling, know that this is part of your Spirit Team in action.

SPIRIT GUIDES

Your Spirit Guides were assigned to you because they are experts on what your soul has come here to achieve and learn. Spirit Guides were once human just like you, but they have learned to raise their consciousness and master the soul lessons that they needed to fulfill. Because Spirit Guides were once human, they have a keen understanding of the physical world and can help you from both an "earthly" level and a spiritual level. Spirit Guides can be animals or a loved one who has crossed over. You can have more than one Spirit Guide, and different Guides may appear in your life during different times and stages.

MY FIRST EXPERIENCE WITH MY SPIRIT GUIDE

When I was around seven or eight years old, I had a beautiful encounter with what I feel was my Spirit Guide. At the time I had no idea exactly what I was encountering, but being in the presence of this higher being was a comforting and loving experience that felt very supportive.

It was the night before I was about to go in for a minor surgery on my foot. Even though the procedure was routine and nothing life-threatening, it was a scary experience for me. I knew they were going to stick a needle into my toe, and I was petrified. As I was trying to fall asleep, I heard the gentle whisper of what sounded like a woman's voice. I didn't see a being appear before me, but I could feel the presence of one standing over my bed. Intuitively I knew this being was there to help me, and from its presence I instantly felt comfortable and understood. It was an amazing feeling of support, comfort, and unconditional love. The being assured me that she was going to protect me and watch out for me during the surgery, and that she would be there to help me.

Because this happened when I was so young, I really didn't think much of it. But I knew the experience was profound. As I grew up, I chalked up this visitor to my silly imagination and forgot all about it. It wasn't until I started on my spiritual awakening journey many years later that I was reconnected with that being and understood that it was one of my Spirit Guides.

Today, I connect and talk to my Spirit Guides whenever I need guidance, reassurance, or help with something. I always feel their presence guiding me, and I have found over the years that the more I am open and trusting to the messages I receive, the stronger they appear in my life.

ANGELS

Angels are revered by many cultures and religions from all corners of the world. They work in a similar way as Spirit Guides; the only difference is that most Angels have not existed in human form before and have only lived in angelic realms. Angels are extremely powerful, positive, and loving beings. In my experience, Angels generally tend to have a slightly different vibrational frequency than Spirit Guides and their presence is often unmistakable. When you encounter an Angel, you most probably will know it right away. Although we all have our own Guardian Angels, Archangels are also here to guide and support everyone. You may have even heard of a few of these Archangels before. Archangel Michael, for example, is one of the most popular. Archangels are accessible to anyone, and they are not aligned with a particular faith or religion. As long as you believe, they are there to help.

HOW TO CONNECT WITH YOUR ANGELS

It's very easy to get in touch with your Angels—simply call on them. All you have to do is speak to them from your heart and trust that they will hear your call.

For example, one day I had lost my favorite pair of earrings. Tearing up my small one-bedroom apartment, I still couldn't find them even though I had searched everywhere. I had once heard that Archangel Michael was the Angel in charge of helping you find lost things, so I called on his help and asked him for his guidance: "Archangel Michael, I am sure you probably have a million better things to do, but can you please help me find my earrings?" I sent out the call and then started cleaning up the mess I had made during my search. A few moments later I walked into my bedroom and there on top of my bedside table was a box of mine that I sometimes kept random pieces of jewelry in. That box definitely was not on my bedside table before I left the room, so it caught my attention. I opened the box and of course, inside it were my earrings. I thanked Archangel Michael, and I have been using his services ever since.

WHAT CAN THEY HELP WITH?

You can call on your Angels to help you with many things, and no problem is too big or too small. Your Angels are there to help you, no matter how insignificant a concern may seem. Angels make no judgments. Of course, when you do ask for their help, whatever the outcome, pay gratitude and thank them right away.

When first starting out, it may be easier to connect with Archangels as you can put a name to them. Here are some calls you can make:

1. **Finding Lost Objects:** Call on Archangel Michael or Archangel Chamuel to help you find lost objects.
2. **Travel Plans:** Call on Archangel Raphael to help ensure that your travel plans run smoothly and safely, and are stress-free.
3. **Well-Being of Your Children or Pets:** Call on Archangel Gabriel to help protect and ease worries surrounding your children or pets.
4. **Important Interviews, Tests, or Meetings:** Call on Archangel Uriel if you need to keep a clear or sharp mind when going in for a meeting, interview, or test.

5. **Money Problems:** Call on Archangel Ariel for guidance when you need help paying your bills, organizing your finances, or when money is owed to you.
6. **Harmonious Relationships:** Call on Archangel Raguel if you are struggling in your relationships, or if you want to increase your feelings of trust, honesty, and love.
7. **Anxiety:** Call on Archangel Jophiel or Archangel Michael to help ease feelings of worry, anxiety, and panic.
8. **Health Issues:** If you need help and guidance with health issues, Archangel Raphael is the one to call for protection and support.
9. **Protection from Negative Energy or Danger:** Call on Archangel Michael for protection and help with fighting off negative energy.

HOW ANGELS AND SPIRIT GUIDES SEND MESSAGES

Guardian Angels and Spirit Guides communicate to us through both subtle and obvious ways. The message you receive may be something as slight as hearing your name called, or the message could be as dramatic as the vision of an Angel standing before you as you avoid a car crash. Angels and Spirit Guides are always operating in our lives in mysterious and not-so-mysterious ways, but you really need to invite them into your life in order to experience the full wonder and bliss of having them by your side.

There are many ways that your Spirit Team can deliver messages to you, and the more open you are to receiving their messages, the more likely you are to hear them. Sometimes messages may come to you in an unexpected way; other times the message may be so soft and quiet that you may have difficulty hearing it unless you are still. Sometimes the message may also be staring right at you in the face, but you could be too closed off or not in the right energetic space to notice it.

Here are some ways that Angels and Spirit Guides deliver messages:

- **Number Patterns:** If you keep seeing the same set of numbers every time you look at the clock or every time you pass a street number, this could indicate that your Angels and Spirit Guides are aiming to make contact with you.
- **Orbs or Light Flickers:** Seeing flashing or sparkling lights out of the corner of your eye could indicate that Angels or Guides are close by. White lights are usually seen when Spirit Guides are present, and colored lights (such as blue) are usually seen when Angels are present.
- **Butterfly, Dragonfly, or Moth:** Seeing one of these delicate creatures is often a sign that your Spirit Guides and Angels are protecting you. It can also be a sign of well-wishes and peace from a loved one who has recently crossed over.
- **A Song/Music:** Hearing faint music or bells, or having a song that comes into your head randomly can also be a message from your Spirit Guides and Angels. Pay attention to the lyrics or how the music makes you feel to determine what message they may be trying to pass over.

- **Your Name:** Hearing your name called when no one else is around is a sign from your Angels or Guides that they have heard and received your wishes. This could also be a sign from your Spirit Team that you need to communicate and get clear about what it is that you want.
- **Automatic Writing:** Feeling the urge to pick up a pen or type out a story, song, or poem can be another sign from your Angels and Guides; these urges often indicate that they are trying to deliver a message or creative inspiration to you.
- **High-Pitched Ringing:** Ruling out medical conditions, when you hear a high-pitched frequency ringing in your ears, this is often a sign that your Spirit Guides or Angels are around and want you to pay close attention to the present situation.
- **Vivid or Recurring Dreams:** Having the same dream over and over again can be a message from your Guides or Angels. To interpret what this may mean, write down the dream and reflect back on it through the next couple of days. It is often your feelings about the dream and not the content that holds the message.

While it is not necessary for you to connect with your Spirit Guides or Angels as you navigate through this life, doing so can truly shift your life to a whole new level. Contacting your Spirit Team provides reassurance and assistance, especially when you are at a crossroads in your life. Making these connections can also be extremely comforting in times of need, helping us feel that we are infinitely supported and protected by something bigger than what we can just see.

Exercise: Connect with Your Spirit Guides and Guardian Angels

Find a quiet place where you can't be disturbed. Sit in a lotus position, sit upright in a chair, or lie down on your bed. Keep your palms facing upward. Close your eyes and take three to four deep breaths to relax your mind and still your heart. Repeat the affirmation *"I am protected, I am loved"* as you continue to breathe. As you recite this affirmation, imagine a white light spreading up through and around your body. Try to release any thoughts that are swimming around in your mind and put them on hold for just a moment. Focus on your breathing to help you with this.

When your mind finally becomes still and calm, begin to ask your Spirit Guides and Angels to come forward to you during the week. You can even ask them to send you a specific sign so you know that they are with you. Invite them into your life with open arms and let them know that they are welcome to guide you.

Close your meditation by saying thank you and sending them gratitude for being in your life. Remain open for the rest of the week and see if you notice the presence of your Spirit Guides or Angels.

HOW TO KNOW WHEN YOU HAVE MADE A CONNECTION

Connecting and tuning in to your Spirit Team is a different experience for everyone, but through practices like meditation and strengthening your intuition, you can start to reach out and make contact. As

I have worked with my Spirit Guides and Angels more and more, I have come to understand that I need only to ask and request their help to receive it. They will always show up to offer support, and I just have to be open to their help. To reach out to them, I simply ask and see what unfolds.

I had a client who, during an intuitive reading, wanted to know how she could connect to her Spirit Guides. She had tried reaching out and asking them to come forward, but she felt as if she wasn't able to hear a clear answer back. As we began talking she shared that she was a songwriter and every time she picked up the pen to write, the words just flowed out of her. The words were so prophetic and so deep that it felt to her like they came from another place. When she shared this with me, I instantly felt confirmation that her Spirit Guides were channeling messages through her songwriting. When I offered her this observation to see if it resonated, she was blown away and instantly had an intuitive feeling that it was true. She was then able to look back through the songs that she had written to determine that her Guides were always there, answering her questions. And even though some of the messages were cryptic, she felt reassured that her Spirit Guides were there helping her through her career as a songwriter.

All Guides communicate differently, so the only way you are going to know if you are receiving clear messages is through your intuition. Guides are always communicating with us, but if you are closed off from this type of energy, you will have a difficult time noticing a message even when it hits you in the face.

Along with being positive and supportive, Spirit Guide messages often feel very similar to intuition. You may feel a strong sense of knowing, or you may receive a strong feeling that seems to hold the answers you have been looking for.

Spirit Guides Aren't Demanding

It is also important to understand that Spirit Guides are not here to tell you exactly how to live your life. They merely offer guidance. Spirit Guides never demand that you do something, nor do they pressure you to act on their guidance. Their words are loving, kind, and gentle. If you feel uplifted by a message you are receiving, count that as another positive sign that you are indeed making contact.

LEARNING HOW TO TRUST THE MESSAGES YOU RECEIVE

You may have difficulty receiving a message when you are in a highly emotional state, or when you are adamant on receiving a message or guidance. This is why when you are first starting out, it is best to reach out to your Spirit Team when you are in a calm and centered place. Your Spirit Team is always there to guide you, but you have to invite them in and be open to receiving their messages. If you are closed off or not trusting of the process, it is going to be very difficult for you to interpret things. Just like when working with your intuition, the most important thing you can do is trust any messages you hear or feel and trust that you are being guided. Sometimes messages from your Spirit Team will be very clear and obvious and other times they may be harder to interpret. Either way, keep trusting yourself and know that you will continue to be guided and supported. If you have received an unclear message, you can also ask your Spirit Team for clarity. Simply ask them to send you a clear and easy to understand sign to help guide you in the right direction. Then stay open and trusting to whatever flows in next. I have often found, when you trust the messages you receive, your connection with your Spirit Team gets stronger and stronger.

EARTH ANGELS

Your Spirit Team doesn't just operate on a Divine level, it operates on a human level as well. Sometimes you encounter people who seem to deliver messages to you, help you out of a situation, or guide you through your own spiritual journey. These people are Earth Angels and appear in human or animal form in your physical reality. Earth Angels often have a very strong presence that can be naturally healing or inspiring. Earth Angels can also present themselves to you when you most need them. Sometimes they stay in your life for a while, and other times they leave as quickly as they came.

MY ENCOUNTER WITH AN EARTH ANGEL

I was walking to the bus stop one morning and was just about to cross the road when a car came speeding through the intersection followed by a trail of police cars.

The speeding car crashed into another car in the intersection and both of them spun across the road. Debris and glass flew everywhere. In that moment, I realized that if I had been any farther across the intersection, I may have been seriously injured. Thankfully no one was hurt, but I was shaken to my core. I stood there unable to move for quite some time, watching the victims emerge from the cars.

I am not sure how long I stood there, but eventually I crossed the road to my bus stop. At the bus stop, I encountered a young man standing there. He had also witnessed the whole thing. He was short with black hair and olive skin, and he instantly asked me if I was okay. I nodded but couldn't say much else. He then opened up a bag of groceries that he was carrying and pulled out a slice of bread. "Carbohydrates are good for shock," he said as he ripped a slice in half. I thanked him and took the bread, but didn't really want to eat it. He just stood there smiling and reassuring me that no one was hurt and everything would be okay. When the bus came he asked me what stop I would be getting off at. Reluctantly I told him. Then he walked up to the bus driver, told the driver to stop at my stop, grabbed his groceries, and walked away.

I was really surprised when he didn't get on the bus as I was sure he was waiting for it too. When I looked back to see which direction he went in, he was gone. I was too shocked to worry about it then, but afterward I couldn't help but wonder about this strange encounter. I felt bad that I hadn't really thanked him, though I figured I would see him again at the same bus stop. But I never did. It wasn't until many months later when I realized that this encounter could have very well been with an Earth Angel.

OPENING THE LINES OF COMMUNICATION

Connecting with your Spirit Guides or Angels is not just about asking for something and then expecting answers. It is more about opening a channel of communication so you can be the best person you can be, and so you can receive guidance and support when you need it.

The quality of your intention when reaching out to your Spirit Guides and Angels is what determines the quality of your connection. If your intention is to truly grow and uplift yourself so that you can connect with the Divine realms, then your Spirit Guides are going to support you with that. But if you are only interested in reaching out but refuse to do the work of opening yourself to receive their help, then it is going to be a lot harder for you to make a connection.

UNDERSTANDING AND LIVING OUT YOUR SOUL CONTRACT

Your soul contract highlights the family that you will be born into and lists any experiences or soulmates that you are destined to meet to help you along your path. Everyone's soul contract looks different and each is uniquely specific to the person and the soul. Before your soul enters into your physical body, it understands that there are specific things that it needs to learn while in that physical form. The things that your soul has chosen to learn in this life stem from past lives, karma, and any other lessons that your soul feels are valuable. These lessons are etched onto your soul contract and dictate part of the map that you will follow in this life. This is not to say that your entire life is predetermined, but there are certain lessons that are destined to be part of your life. How these lessons manifest are up to the decisions and choices that you make once you come to earth.

To help you with these lessons, you are assigned a Spirit Team who will help guide you along the way. Your soul also gets to choose which family it wants to be born into. The family your soul chooses holds a lot of the lessons and energy that your soul has come here to experience. Your soul may have also been able to choose other elements of its destiny as well. This destiny is indicated on your soul contract, and every soul that comes to earth has signed such a contract.

Reading Your Contract

It is possible to see what is written on your soul contract. Often this is what a psychic may be tuning in to when she gives you a reading or what a palm reader or astrologer may be looking at when he sees your hand or your horoscope. However, seeing your soul contract is never going to replace actually living it.

Even though your soul contract is a "contract," there is no punishment or judgment if you don't complete a lesson. This contract is more of an energetic map that highlights some of the bigger themes in your life and what your soul has come here to achieve. You can get some hint as to what is on your soul contract by the lessons and people that are presented to you in your life. You may be able to notice a recurring theme, or perhaps you are able to identify certain patterns that seem to operate within your family. Because families share so much energy, you may be able to see some of the life lessons that you are destined to experience by observing the members of your family.

YOU CHOSE YOUR FAMILY

Even though family can feel frustrating at times, their souls are crucial to your growth and development. They are often your most powerful teachers and students. The family that you were born into is no mistake. Your soul chose your family because it knew it was the perfect family for it to learn the lessons that it needed to learn. During the first eight years of your life, your subconscious mind was being programmed. The thoughts, feelings, resources, and tools that filled your mind were mostly inherited from your family. Your family also provided you with the DNA, which contains your energetic code for materializing into human form. All of this, when combined, gives rise to the shell that your soul needs in order to learn its lessons and grow.

It is important to understand that your soul has come here to experience the sheer bliss and joy that is felt through growth. Your family gave you all the tools you needed to grow, and this holds true whether you were adopted or if one or more of your parents were absent from your life. Regardless, the energy that your parents passed down to you is a critical component of your soul's evolutionary purpose.

Sometimes it is your soul's job to bring an end to family patterns that have existed for generations. Often when you are able to transcend and heal family patterns, you don't just heal them for yourself, but you also heal them for everyone else in the family and the generations that follow.

If you find yourself following in the footsteps of another family member, it could be that your soul has come to progress that energy so it can continue being evolved and manifested into the world.

YOUR SOUL CONTRACT HELPS YOU REACH YOUR POTENTIAL

Even though we all have a soul contract, our future is not completely set in stone. Some events in our lives are perhaps predetermined, but many other facets are not. In fact, your soul contract is more about potential than about specific events laid out in detail.

We all come into this life with a set of energetic potentials. When your soul came to this earth, it came equipped with all the necessary tools that it needed in order to fulfill its purpose. These tools are like seeds; they exist only as potentials and need to be nurtured, recognized, and nourished in order to blossom. These seeds are part of your life purpose and are part of the path that your soul is destined to take. Some of us will plant and harvest all the seeds that we were given, and some of us will only plant a few. Neither way is better or worse than the other, it is all just part of the journey and part of the cycle of growth.

When you become aware of the nature of the Universe and the amazing, magical potential that is inside you and all around you, it becomes a lot easier to start planting these seeds. When the fear melts away and you find freedom in your heart and mind, you will be able to trust that the seeds will grow. When you can experience the bountiful harvests of all the seeds you have planted, you are walking the highest path. Recall that the highest path is not a destination; it is a state of mind. The highest path is a state of mind that allows every single flower in your garden to bloom.

REMEMBERING YOUR CONNECTION TO THE EARTH

We all have a responsibility to Mother Earth. When you came into this life, part of your soul contract was to look after the well-being of this planet and be responsible for its upkeep. Because we are all connected, and all made from the same energy at our core, everything on this planet is essentially us, everything is an extension of who we are. Every living thing on this planet is part of the bigger tapestry of where we have come from and where we will return. You may feel this when out in nature; you may feel this when a gentle breeze caresses your face. You may feel this as the snowy winter colors your cheeks and tickles your nose.

CONNECTING TO NATURE IN MODERN TIMES

Nature is always speaking to us and is always reacting with us. Science has even found that nature is healing to the body. The ancients used nature as their guide. They worshipped the Sun and the stars, and they used nature to guide them in the right direction. Before Wi-Fi and the creation of the Internet, before the advent of modern civilization, nature offered the only "connections" we needed. Many tribes would use the trees to communicate messages throughout the forest. They did this by understanding the energy fields of the trees. Just like you have your own energy field, so do trees and so does every other living thing. By connecting with this energy field they were able to telepathically receive information from the trees. This may seem far-fetched, but only as far-fetched as explaining the amazing marvel that is the Internet to an ancient tribe!

In this modern era, it is easy to forget about the significance of nature. We forget about the calming and healing effects that nature can bring us. When we tune in to the Universe, however, and tune in to the feeling of the Sun on our face, or the full Moon on a dark night, we feel moved. We feel stirred by these things. And this is because we are all connected.

TAKING CARE OF THE PLANET

Everyone wants to change the world and make it a better place, but the only way you can really do that with lasting impact is to first take responsibility for yourself and the pollution that you put out into the world. This is not just pollution in the form of greenhouse gases and carbon emissions; it also includes energetic pollution. Your every thought and every action carries an energy that is sent out into the world. Your energy is either contributing to the energetic pollution of the environment or is contributing to the nurturing and healing of the environment. If you are putting hostile thoughts out into the world, if you are always focusing on the negative and terrible things that are happening, in many ways you are feeding this energy. The world doesn't need your pity, the world doesn't need your anger, the world needs your healing and loving energy.

Whenever you speak or take an action, you are dictating what type of world you want to live in. The more hateful your thoughts and the more hateful actions you take, the more hate you are putting out into the world. Conversely, the more loving your actions and the more loving words you speak, the more love you are putting out into the world. At any moment, your energy is helping to shift this planet into a higher level of consciousness and a more loving place, or into a lower level of consciousness and a more fear-filled place.

We all have to start taking responsibility for our energy. We have to stop focusing on what other people are doing and all the negativity that is in the world, and instead we need to focus on what we can do to bring light and healing into the world. Doing so doesn't have to be a big or grand act; in fact it really is quite simple. If you want to change the world, if you really want to make a difference, start by taking responsibility for the energy that you put out into the world. Whatever you feed yourself with, you are also feeding the world. This is a big responsibility, but you are strong enough to handle it.

As part of our soul contract, we have all promised to care for and look after this planet. We have all promised to take responsibility for ourselves and our actions, and how can we not? Since we are all connected, when we hurt the planet we are hurting ourselves too. When someone else feels pain, we feel it too. We are all in this together, but instead of getting caught up in everyone else's business and what they are doing wrong or what they are doing right, we have to instead pay attention to ourselves. If more of us can become aware that we are contributing to the state of society and the condition of the world we live in, then we will have a better opportunity to make a difference for the better. When everyone can step up and be mindful of the energy they send out into the world, then the world will know true peace.

CHAPTER WRAP-UP

All around us are higher realms of Divine energy which are home to our Spirit Team. Everyone has a Spirit Team, which is made up of your Higher Self, intuition, Angels, Spirit Guides, and higher beings like Archangels. Your Spirit Team is there to guide, support, and protect you on your journey whether you consciously realize it or not. In order to welcome this Divine energy into your life, all you need to do is ask.

- Unlocking your potential is about living an authentic life that feels good from the inside out. To access this, you have to tap into your Higher Self. Your Higher Self is essentially the most authentic version of you and is aligned with your highest path.
- The Universe is always on your side and is always sending you signs and clues to guide you to your highest path.
- To access your Spirit Team, just ask and then remain open to the signs and guidance that follows. The more you trust the connection, the stronger the messages will appear.
- Your Spirit Guides and Angels are there to help and guide you no matter what the problem—there is no problem too big or too small.
- Your Spirit Team is there to guide you as you fulfill your soul contract.
- You chose your family before you came into this life because they contained the energy and DNA that you most needed to live out your soul contract.
- Even though you have a soul contract, you also have free will and are in charge of how you choose to live your life.
- We all have a responsibility to care for the planet, both physically and energetically.

CHAPTER 10

HEAL YOUR MIND, BODY, AND SOUL

There is an unmistakable twinkle in the eyes of those who have found peace in their heart, stillness in their mind, and love in their soul.

POSITIVE MIND, POSITIVE BODY

When you start thinking positively about yourself and the life around you, your entire body glows. With a "can do" attitude, there is nothing you can't achieve and no setback in life that is too great to overcome. This is especially true when it comes to the health and well-being of your body. No one is immune to falling sick; whether it is simply battling the flu or facing a more complicated illness. Illness is something we all have to deal with at some point in our lives. However, with a positive mindset and the wisdom to know the true strength of your body, it can become easier for you to feel good, no matter what health condition you may be dealing with.

> *"If you have good thoughts, they will*
> *shine out of your face like sunbeams*
> *and you will always look lovely."*
>
> —Roald Dahl

Hippocrates, who is known as the father of medicine, believed in the principle of *vis medicatrix naturae*, which translates to the healing power of nature. He understood that the body contained its own self-healing energy and had its own ability to protect itself from disease. He believed that disease and illness could be cured through strengthening the natural healing power of the body. Both modern and traditional medicine is based on this foundation, but it is easy to forget that your body does indeed have these superpowers. Your body's self-healing ability is activated by:

- Disease and illness itself (this stimulates the immune system and helps your body to take action against fighting disease)

- Positive thinking and a "can do" attitude
- Surgeries and other treatments like acupuncture
- Prescribed drugs, vaccines, and herbal medicines
- A nutritious diet loaded with vitamins and minerals
- Energy healing such as crystal therapy, reiki, pranic healing, etc.
- Exercise and stretching
- Spending time in nature

While medical professionals may know the best prescription for your physical body, the best prescription for your mental and emotional health is positive energy. The more positive you can be about your outlook on life and the better you can get at managing your stress levels, the more likely you are to keep your energy and the healing power of your body in tip-top shape.

TAMING STRESS AND ANXIETY

Few of the thoughts in your head are actually very necessary. In fact, if you suffer from regular bouts of stress and anxiety, often the main causes are the thoughts in your mind and not your situation or environment. We all have voices in our head that are constantly chatting and giving us their opinion. These pesky voices are a product of both your conscious and subconscious mind, and learning how to tame these voices is crucial if you want to live a life that is aligned with positive energy.

Understanding the different voices of your mind may help you disengage from your thoughts more completely. Your objective is to learn how to operate from the voice that makes you feel positive, relaxed, and joyful, and hence quiet the voice that makes you feel anxious, stressed, and confused. In many ways, it is like we have two distinct voices in our minds, the voice of the ego and the voice of the heart.

Meditation

Meditation is such a valuable tool for those who suffer from stress and anxiety because it teaches how not to engage with thoughts. While meditating, you are encouraged to align with your true self and shift back into observer mode. You are not your thoughts, which means that when anxious or stressful thoughts arise, you are able to disengage from them. Achieving this level of awareness takes practice, but through regular meditation you can start to tame the thoughts of your mind and allow them to work for you and not against you.

THE VOICE OF THE EGO

The voice of the ego is the voice of survival mode. We need our ego voice to warn us against danger, create boundaries, and rationalize things. Without conscious awareness, the voice of the ego is often the more powerful of the two voices, and it can overrule the voice of the heart. The voice of the ego is also heavily conditioned by society, past experiences, culture, and fear. Because the voice of the ego is designed to protect you, it is often also responsible for those self-limiting beliefs mentioned elsewhere in the book. The ego mind is designed to keep you safe, but it can also become extremely overpowering and cause you to be caught up in a web of fear. The ego voice also:

- Loves to talk about wants and plans
- Enjoys worry and stress
- Likes to think of the worst possible scenario
- Is often quick to judge
- Loves to be right
- Is extremely competitive
- Feeds off of playing the victim

By doing these things, the ego voice can keep you safe from feelings, from getting hurt emotionally, and from physical injury.

The only problem is that when left untamed, the ego voice can also hold you back, close you off from living the life that you deserve, keep you stuck and stagnant, and cause you to lose sight of who you really are.

The ego voice also likes to make you think that you are not enough and that you have to fit in or conform in order to survive. Although we all want to find our place in the world, the ego voice can become so powerful that it forgets to work with the wisdom of the heart. We need our ego in order to survive in this world; however, we also have to get our ego to work alongside the voice of the heart. Many of us forget this, which causes our ego voice to take over, dominate, and leave us feeling gripped by stress and anxiety.

THE VOICE OF THE HEART

The voice of the heart is the voice of compassion and the voice of your dreams, hopes, and wishes. The voice of the heart is a lot quieter than the ego, which means in order to hear the heart, you have to allow your mind to become still. While the ego voice feeds off repetitive thoughts that swim around in your mind, the voice of the heart often communicates to you through compassionate feelings, daydreams, and fantasies. In order to interpret these messages of your heart, you have to create a still environment in your mind that is free of thought.

When the voice of the heart speaks, often you feel instantly calm, hopeful, and inspired. The voice of the heart also:

- Helps bring you back into alignment with unconditional love
- Reminds you that there is always more to the story than you can see at any moment
- Is gentle, loving, and builds you up by making you feel good and reminding you that you are worthy
- Supports and encourages you to dream bigger, think more abundantly, and to focus on the positive
- Helps you to unlock your passions and go after your dreams and desires
- Stimulates your creativity that, in turn, helps improve your ability to problem solve

The voice of the heart is an extremely powerful tool and by accessing this voice, you can begin to shift the way that you move through life.

HOW TO ACCESS THE VOICE OF THE HEART

In order to access the voice of the heart, you first have to still the thoughts in your mind so that you can welcome in the softer guidance of the heart. When your ego voice is yelling at full volume, it becomes very difficult for the heart to have room to speak. Ways to quiet and still your mind include deep breathing, meditation, exercise, dancing, listening to music, gardening, and working on creative projects. In fact, any activity that helps you feel good, stop thinking, and lose track of time can allow the voice of the heart to shine through. Becoming open to the voice of your heart takes practice, but the less you engage the voice of the ego and the more you clear your mind, the easier it will be.

THE EGO AND THE HEART WORKING TOGETHER

You need both the voice of the ego and the voice of the heart to navigate through this dimension. To get the two voices working together, you have to create space for the voice of your heart to send you inspiration, messages, and ideas; and then you have to use the voice of your ego to put those inspirational messages and ideas into action. In many ways, the voice of your heart gives you the passion and creativity to come up with ideas, while the voice of your ego helps you to actually create a plan to put those ideas into action. It may not always work in a process that is as linear as this, but the more you can be aware of which voice is in control at a given time, the easier it will be for you to balance the two.

For example, say you are debating on the direction of a decision that you need to make. When the ego mind is in control, it will start laying out all the facts and information. It will then start sending out a stream of thoughts about every possibility, especially the bad ones, and every little bit of detail. These thoughts may go around and around in your mind for a while, but chances are even if you land on a decision, the ego voice will start making you doubt yourself or will deliver more facts and information that you hadn't yet considered.

This overload of information may cause you to feel confused about which way to turn.

Instead, if you quiet your mind and begin tuning in to the voice of your heart, you may start to daydream about the scenario that you really desire, or feel supported to make a decision from a place of love, rather than fear. The voice of your heart may also inspire you to see things differently, which can help you take into consideration the bigger picture. Once you have received this message from your heart, you can then use your ego voice to start putting plans into place and working out the next steps so as to follow through on your chosen decision.

While not all situations are going to be as clear-cut as this, you may be surprised just how easy and stress free your life becomes when you start to lead with the voice of your heart rather than the voice of your ego.

THE HEALING POWER OF YOUR BODY

There are two main reasons why physical illness becomes present in your body:

1. One reason is that illness is part of your soul contract and part of what your soul has come here to learn. (As hard as this can be to fathom, sometimes the soul has to experience certain things, not because it is being punished, but because through experiencing these things it is able to bring healing and growth to itself and the world.)

2. The other reason that illness takes over your body is because your soul is trying to get your attention. This is especially true when you are facing one of those "mystery" illnesses that don't seem to have a rational or easily identifiable cause.

For an illness to manifest, it first has to occur on an energetic or vibrational level. After illness begins manifesting on an energetic/vibrational level, it then moves to an emotional level, and finally, to a physical level. Because illness is present on an energetic level first, sometimes the only way to get to the root of the problem is to discover the energy disturbance that is causing it. When illness gets to the point that it is manifesting in physical form, often it has been around for some time and the energy disturbance can no longer be suppressed. This energy disturbance needs to be brought up to the surface in order to bring to your attention that something is not right.

BALANCING MODERN MEDICINE WITH LISTENING TO YOUR BODY

In our modern era, we have perhaps become too reliant on popping a pill for every ache, pain, or sensation. While medications can definitely provide relief, they often do not solve the root problem or provide a lasting solution; all they do is mask your ability to understand the problem and learn what your body is trying to tell you. Even though advancements in modern medicine are truly incredible and can be lifesaving, it is important to pay attention to what your body may be trying to communicate to you and then work on addressing the root of the problem rather than just fixing the symptoms.

Make no mistake, while drugs can help you, you also have to be prepared to do some of the work on an energetic, mental, and spiritual level. More often than not, it is your emotions and vibration that is the root cause of disease. More often than not, disease is a sign that your body, mind, and soul are trying to tell you that something is not right, that you need to change something or do something different to bring yourself back into equilibrium.

For example, let's say you have been diagnosed with type 2 diabetes. Your doctor is not surprised because you tell him that your diet basically consists of chocolate cake, cookies, and sugary pastries. The doctor's investigation ends right there, and your diet is pinpointed as being the culprit. While this is accurate, it is only a half-truth. Let's take a closer look at what really may be going on here. The diabetes has already taken hold of your body, so you go on medication and start a healthy diet. This causes you to feel miserable. Your new diet is tough after living off sugar for so long, and the medication is giving you a host of side effects. You struggle to stick to your eating plan, and so you end up going back to your usual dietary habits while taking the medication to keep things in check. Sound familiar? The majority of people who go on medications for chronic illnesses, whether the medications are for cholesterol, diabetes, blood pressure, pain management, and so on, encounter a similar situation.

Now, are you lazy for not changing your eating habits? Are you wanting to create more health problems for yourself? No. Deep down, you have not been able to get to the root of the real problem. What is really going on with your sugar addiction? As it turns out, often sugar addictions are linked to feelings of low self-esteem and a lack of self-worth. Your sugar addiction started perhaps during a stressful period in your life, and you began eating sugary foods in order to avoid certain feelings or emotions about the situation. Perhaps now you can see why your diet is only half of the problem, the other half of the issue is why your diet was so out of balance in the first place. When you dig a little deeper and discover the root cause of disease on an emotional level, it will always help in the treatment of it and may even lead to the cure.

ADDICTION AND ENERGY

The same principle can be applied to people who have other types of addictions. There is no excuse nowadays not to know that smoking kills and yet millions still do smoke. These people are physically addicted, of course, and chances are they will remain addicted until they are able to get to the root of what has caused their addiction in the first place. People gravitate toward vices like tobacco, sugar, and so on when they are out of alignment with themselves and with their souls. But when you raise your vibration and start filling your life with positive energy, often your addiction, or the action that is causing the illness to manifest, melts away and becomes very easy to tame. This is because the addiction and action no longer vibrationally align with the positive energy that you are emitting.

DISEASE IS JUST DIS-EASE

When you align with your true self and reconnect with your soul then disease, addiction, and illness often become a lot easier to manage. Sometimes they even dissipate from your life altogether. Our bodies are not designed to do things that will injure us or cause disease. Our bodies are not designed to overeat or to crave foods that provide no nutritional value. Our bodies are not designed to develop diabetes or other illnesses. What drives these things to happen is being out of alignment with your mind, body and soul. You start these disease-causing habits when you are in avoidance of who you really are and when you are living from a place of fear, worry, and stress. This is why it is so important to look at the emotional cause or energetic disturbance behind an illness.

Integrative Medicine

Integrative medicine is an emerging field that aims to treat the whole patient on all levels: physical, mental, emotional, and spiritual. Integrative health practitioners use a combination of modern medicine and natural therapies including herbs, acupuncture, and so on. Due to the increase in people turning to natural healing therapies, more and more doctors are starting to employ this type of healthcare in their practices.

Even though you may have access to everything modern medicine has to offer, it is important that you not forget your own healing power and the value of looking beneath the surface to see what is really going on. When you approach your health in this way, when you approach your health from a mind-body-soul perspective, it will change the way you view disease completely. You will come to understand that disease is simply "dis-ease." And when you can address what is causing you to feel out of alignment and look into that cause, then you may find that whatever it is that ails you disappears, as if by magic.

MIRACULOUS HEALINGS

There are countless stories about miracle healings and the spontaneous disappearance of disease. These stories however, are often meaningless unless you have witnessed them for yourself. If you are out of touch with the idea that magic and miracles are happening every day, then you might find it difficult to fathom that they even really exist. These so-called miracles are often a product of spiritual or emotional healing that causes patients to shift their mindsets and lifestyles, and take control over their own health. Sometimes these miracles are even the result of positive thinking, or they come about because the patient reached out to Divine guidance for help.

Growing up, I had a dear friend who suffered from epilepsy. Although her seizures were quite rare, when they happened she would be gone from school for a long time. One day after a particular bad seizure, she returned to school fairly shortly after. I didn't really question it too much then, but I do remember noticing how energetic and healthy she seemed. Usually after she returned to school following a seizure, she had this trepidation and cautious energy to her, but this time was definitely different.

In fact, my friend never experienced a seizure ever again.

It wasn't until years later when we were discussing the power of healing that my friend decided to share with me what happened to her that night of her last seizure. She could often feel a seizure coming on, so on this night instead of getting panicked about it she decided to pray. She kept praying and praying, hoping that it would go away and that she would be cured. The seizure ended up coming on anyway, but as she was having her seizure she noticed a brilliant golden light standing before her. She felt an amazing angelic presence comforting her and soothing her, almost like this presence was healing her. She never shared her story with anyone in her family and especially not the doctors, but that was the last seizure she ever had. When I heard this story, it definitely seemed to me that a miraculous healing had taken place. Who is to say why this happened or how it happened. Certainly her healing could very well be chalked up to nothing but a coincidence, but in her mind she knew that she had been healed by a Divine being.

THE MIND-BODY-SOUL CONNECTION

When you realize the powerful connection between the mind, the body, and the soul, you can really start to enter into a place of healing. When this level of awareness is reached and a solution is found for each level of being, miracle healings often occur. It is important to remember, however, that everyone has their own healing journey and their own process to go through. You cannot compare your healing journey to others or push what worked for you onto someone else.

Healing also doesn't necessarily mean that you are free of all symptoms, as healing can happen on many levels and in its own timing. Sometimes simply viewing your disease as an opportunity to get in touch with your mind, body, and soul allows you to feel more at peace with your situation. When it comes to your own healing journey, your path is yours alone. Everyone has a different path. The most important thing you can do is honor yourself, accept yourself as you are, and know that you are a capable, powerful healer who is worthy of being healed. At the end of the day, if your mind is free and you feel good about yourself regardless of your condition, perhaps that is all the healing you need.

Exercise: Steps to Taking a Mind-Body-Soul Approach to Healing

If you want to start looking at the energetic and emotional side of disease and get in touch with your body, here are some steps you can take:

1. Drop any expectations of what your healing is supposed to look like and keep an open mind. Healing can happen on different levels and may not occur in the way that you expect. You need to remain open to all possibilities.
2. You have to be completely willing and ready to be healed. Sometimes having an illness or disease can allow you to stay in victim mode. This mode may keep you in your comfort zone or in a state of fear, which prevents you from truly living your life. But for true healing to occur you have to be willing to let this go.
3. Make a list of all the feelings and emotions that having this disease stirs within you. How does having this disease make you feel? Really allow yourself to go deep and write down every thought or feeling that you are experiencing.
    a. Now that you have this list in front of you, assess the other things in your life that may be causing you to feel the same way. Assess when these emotions started appearing in your life. Did they come about just because of the disease or were you feeling them before the disease began manifesting physically?

These emotions could very well hold a clue as to how or why this disease manifested.

   b. See if you can put measures in place to start addressing some of the key emotions that you wrote down. For example, if you are feeling anger try to bring more acceptance or loving energy into your life. If a few things are causing you to feel angry in your life, try confronting them or find new ways to see them.

4. Practice self-love and acceptance, as these are wonderful healing tools that can instantly bring peace to your situation. Accept all of your signs and symptoms, and instead of focusing on your illness start focusing on the parts of you that are feeling well and vibrant.

5. If you want to flex your intuitive muscles, you may even want to talk to your disease. Ask it why it is there and try to discover what message your body is trying to communicate to you.

6. Ask your Angels, Spirit Guides, or Higher Self to help you activate your body's own self-healing ability. Stay open to the signs and messages that you receive and trust in the process.

When you use these steps in conjunction with advice from a medical professional, you tap into the amazing power that lives within you and healing can occur on all levels of your being.

CHAPTER WRAP-UP

Your body contains its own powerful healing ability. Just like your skin magically heals when you cut yourself, your entire body has the ability to heal as long as it is supported on a physical, emotional, mental, and spiritual level. Disease can simply be looked at as dis-ease, and by finding the root cause, whether it is emotional, spiritual, or physical, it can help to heal your body from the inside out.

- Stress and anxiety can wreak havoc on the body. To reduce stress and anxiety, you need to learn how to tame the voices in your mind.
- Learning how to work with the voice of the heart and the ego is important for living a well-rounded and balanced life.
- Your body contains an immense ability to heal itself; in order to activate your own healing ability, you have to approach your health from a mind-body-soul perspective.
- Disease and illness happen to all of us. It is important to understand that disease is not a sign of "failure" or that you did something wrong; rather, it is an opportunity to listen to your body a little more closely and learn to nourish and love it just that little bit more.
- Medical professionals can only do part of the healing; the rest of the healing has to come from you.
- Healing yourself is about accepting and loving yourself and about addressing any spiritual or emotional symptoms that may be present.
- Everyone's healing journey looks different; you don't have to be cured to be healed. True healing is all about your mindset.

CHAPTER 11

POSITIVE ENERGY, POSITIVE LIFE

When you understand the power of aligning your life with positive energy, you will have in your hands the answer to every question, the key to unlock every door, and the tools to create unlimited joy in your life.

SHIFTING YOUR LIFE TAKES TIME

If you have been operating with self-limiting or negative thoughts for most of your life, it is going to take time before you start noticing the profound shift that positive energy can bring. In fact, in the beginning you are going to need to work hard on reprogramming your mind and reconditioning your old belief systems and values. Once you have mastered this work, aligning with positive energy will be your natural state of being, and the process will feel effortless.

It is important that throughout this process you practice being gentle and loving with yourself. If you notice negative or self-limiting thoughts arising, do not resist them. Instead, simply allow them to flow in without engaging them. You can also shift these thoughts into something more loving and supportive. Doing so will help you realign and come back to a place of positivity. Think of it like you are conditioning your mind to become your best friend, your biggest fan, and your strongest support system. This process may take time and you will encounter some resistance or hurdles along the way, but that is all part of the process. The more often you can keep bringing your mindset back to positivity, the more graceful, easy, and joyous your life is going to become.

YOU DESERVE A POSITIVE LIFE

When your soul came to this earth, it knew that it came for a joyous adventure full of opportunities, growth, laughter, and excitement. Your life is an amazing journey that is part of a much bigger picture and a much bigger cycle of events. Getting caught up on the little things, taking your life too seriously, and stressing is such a waste of time and only prevents you from living the blissful life that you so deserve. Every opportunity that comes your way is an opportunity for you to learn, for you to grow, and for you to explore a different side of you and a different side of your life.

Whenever opportunities come your way, you have a choice over how you are going to handle them. Either you can:

1. Get swallowed up by them and allow them to consume your life, or you can
2. Embrace them and trust that your experiences are just part of a learning process that is itself part of a much bigger picture

When you choose to embrace whatever life is offering you, you will feel at ease about your life and be open to accepting the many blessings that life is always offering you. If you are always caught up in the victim mindset, stressing about every little thing, or getting caught up in drama, it is going to be very difficult for you to open yourself up to the amazing power and potential that is all around you and inside of you.

It is your birthright to live in joy. It is your birthright to live a life that feels inspired. And if you don't feel this way about your life, the only person who can change things is you. You get what you deserve in this life, but if you are constantly beating yourself up and putting yourself down, then you will only be delivering more of these experiences into your life. When you start loving yourself again, when you start shifting to a place of positive energy, the Universe responds to that and starts sending you opportunities and circumstances that reflect your mindset. You deserve to be happy and you deserve to live a life that feels fulfilling. But you first have to believe that you deserve these things for these things to be delivered to you.

OWN YOUR HAPPINESS

Everything that you ever need for yourself is inside of you, not outside of you. You are never going to find happiness in external things, be it objects or people. Sure, these things may provide you with a temporary sliver of happiness, but true happiness has to be created from within. When you can be happy with whatever circumstances come your way, when you can be happy with whatever life brings for you, then you can meet all challenges and obstacles from a place of freedom and courage.

Happy People Still Have Problems

Happy people don't have perfect lives with no troubles; happy people have just learned how to prevent their troubles from getting the better of them. You will always be faced with challenges in life, but the deeper and stronger you make your connection to your soul, the easier it will be for you to move through difficult situations when they occur.

You are responsible for your own happiness and you are the creator of your own happiness. No one can create or offer you happiness; that job is solely your responsibility. In order to create more happiness in your life, you first have to start feeling genuinely happy for all that you have. When you can find the small instances of happiness in every single day or in every single moment, a snowball effect occurs where more happiness and more happy thoughts come your way. If you have been miserable or depressed for a long time, you may struggle to reach for a happy thought. But even if you start slow, even if you just take a small step forward each day, you can make enough progress to get on the right track.

"Happiness is letting go of what you think your life is supposed to look like and celebrating it for everything that it is."

—Mandy Hale

Your intention means everything. If you truly want to be happy, if you truly want to reach for happy thoughts, if you truly want to get up and out of your funk and into a place of happiness, then you are going to find the way eventually. The more you believe in yourself and the more you claim your personal power, the easier it is going to be for you to create whatever it is that you desire for yourself, including more happiness.

DON'T TRY TOO HARD: JUST BE

It is a very exciting thing to learn that you have the power to co-create an amazing life for yourself. You are far more powerful than you realize; your thoughts and vibration are responsible for what you attract into your life. This can be an awe-inspiring revelation, and when you discover all of this you might be tempted to shift into a place of wanting to be nothing but positive, or wanting to be more aware all the time, or wanting to be all of these "things" all day, every day. While being these things are all well and good, this pursuit can sometimes inadvertently throw you off course. It is far more powerful to understand and comprehend these things and then allow yourself to just be.

Every piece of advice and every exercise in this book is there to help you get back to who you really are so that you can reconnect with your true, authentic self. You don't have to *try* to be more of this or less of this; all you need to do is be. Pure and simple.

Even though it may seem somewhat counterintuitive, amazing things can happen when you stop trying and just allow yourself to be as you are. Being in a place of complete nonresistance automatically shifts you into alignment and allows you to start operating from a place of positive energy. Take all of this information deep into your soul, sit with it, and then just allow it to be. Allow yourself to be just as you are. Your only responsibility in this life is to be true to you and true to your own energy. Drop any expectations and instead allow yourself to rise up and be who you really are. Shift your mindset from being this or that, and simply just be.

BE CAREFUL WITH EXPECTATIONS

Many of us have expectations that we carry around, but expectations can sometimes get us stuck and out of alignment with what messages the Universe or our soul is trying to send us. When we have expectations, it is very difficult for us to be open to anything new and can close us off from unexpected opportunities. While it is reasonable to have some expectations in life, be mindful of the expectations you are placing on yourself and others. Are these expectations serving you or are they causing you to feel closed off? When your expectations are not met, you might experience a lot of disappointment, anger, and even pain. Having unmet expectations can cause you to instantly slip into a negative mindset, which lowers your vibration. Life doesn't often go to plan or unfold as expected, so perhaps you can experience less stress and less disappointment if you just remove expectations and instead go with the flow. When you trust and join the flow of life without expectations, you allow yourself to appreciate more and see things as they really are. The same goes for your relationships: When you drop expectations that you place on other people and you join the flow, then you will be better able to see people for who they really are and allow everyone involved to be more comfortable in being themselves.

We must be especially careful with the expectations we put on our romantic partners. In reality you are the only person who is ever going to make you feel whole, but our society often tells us otherwise. Many Hollywood movies, for example, tells us that our partner needs to "complete" us and make us whole. This mentality can sometimes leave you with a laundry list of expectations that you place on your partner—they should look like this, they should do this, they should know exactly what I want when I want it! Sometimes, the expectations we have for others are so lofty that we cannot even live up to them ourselves! While it is fair to have some expectations like respect, trust, and so on, all the other ego stuff can block the relationship and make it harder for you (and your partner) to feel loved and accepted.

THE WISDOM OF "IS THAT SO?"

There is a famous story of a Buddhist monk who would only reply "Is that so?" to whatever experiences came his way. The monk had reached such a level of consciousness and awareness that it only seemed natural to him to simply accept whatever it was that came his way without resistance. One day, the monk was accused of getting a girl in the local village pregnant. The father of the girl was furious and demanded that the monk look after the baby and provide for it. Even though the accusations were false, the monk simply replied "Is that so?" and took the baby into his care. He never argued or pleaded his innocence; he simply accepted. By accepting the baby, many of the villagers assumed he was guilty and shunned him from the community.

Exercise: Practice "Is That So?"

Just for a moment repeat the words "Is that so?" to yourself a few times. What feelings do these words evoke for you? "Is that so?" is a mark of freedom, a mark of being completely accepting of every given moment without judgment and without attachment. Practicing the "Is that so?" philosophy does not require that you don't stand up for yourself or assert yourself, instead it is about bringing acceptance to each moment, no matter what arises. When you can approach situations without confrontation or resistance, they are often resolved more easily and with less stress and hostility. When you take a calm approach, solutions are easier to find and often things begin shifting into alignment on their own. Remember, the more aligned you are on the inside, the more alignment will be reflected back to you on the outside.

The girl who accused the monk watched his behavior and began to feel extremely guilty. Eventually she came forward to the monk and admitted the truth. Again, the monk simply replied "Is that so?" and handed the baby back to her.

While we may not be able to reach the same level of enlightenment or detachment as this monk, there is something we can all take away from this story. When you have no expectations from others, from life, and from the world, when you simply accept whatever it is that comes your way and embrace it, then you allow yourself to enter into a new state of freedom and a more relaxed and centered way of being.

THE LONG-TERM BENEFITS OF POSITIVE ENERGY

When you start to bring positive energy into your life and this force starts to grow, you are going to begin noticing changes on the inside first and then changes on the outside. The inside changes often occur on a subtle level and it is likely that only you will notice the shifts. With the passage of time however, the effects of positive energy are going to start trickling into your physical reality and into your environment. For example:

- People may comment that you look different, and your eyes may appear brighter.
- People may notice your energy and feel drawn to you without knowing why.
- You might attract more like-minded people.
- You may find it more challenging to tolerate people or situations that are negative.
- Your energy may become more sensitive, and you may pick up vibrations around you and from other people.
- You may organically change the way you dress, the way you eat, and the way you hold and carry yourself.

These are the benefits of awakening to the power of positive energy. As you reach the last few pages of this book, it is very likely that you will start noticing these effects.

SIGNS THAT YOUR ENERGY IS ASCENDING

As you begin aligning your life with positive energy and raising your vibration, you may start to notice particular signs or symptoms. These signs and symptoms are often the product of an energy shift or a cleansing process that occurs to help your life rise to a new vibrational level. This is called ascension. When your energy begins ascending and raising to a higher vibration, you may notice the following:

- **Difficulty sleeping or a disruption of your regular sleeping patterns:** Through the ascension process, old emotions, thoughts, and feelings are likely to bubble to the surface in order to be cleared. This can cause an overactive mind and make it harder for you to sleep. Waking up between 3 a.m. and 5 a.m. may also happen during the ascension process and is a sign that your creative energy is increasing.
- **Feeling emotional:** During the ascension process your energy is extremely sensitive, which can cause you to feel emotions on a much deeper level. Releasing blocks from your life can also make accessing your emotions a lot easier.
- **Increased sensitivity to sounds and colors:** The ascension process causes you to see colors more brightly and vividly because your perception of the world is changing. You may also become more sensitive to sounds and your taste in music may even change.
- **Desire to change your diet:** During the ascension process heavy foods like meat may cause you to feel sluggish or out of balance. You may also find that you are naturally drawn to

eating a plant-based diet or raw foods that have an "aliveness" to them.

- **Heightened perception of other people's feelings:** As your sensitivity increases, it is common to start feeling the emotions of other people and your environment. It may also become more difficult for you to be in large crowds or around certain people.
- **Vivid or prophetic dreams:** As your vibration starts rising, your dreams become clearer and may even start communicating messages to you.
- **Feeling energy:** An exercise at the start of the book showed you how to feel the energy of your soul by rubbing your hands together and slowly moving them apart. Now that you have read this far and have been doing the work, is it easier for you to feel your energy?
- **Increased intuition:** As you raise your level of awareness, you will be able to open your third eye and start receiving and interpreting intuitive messages more accurately.
- **An increase in synchronistic events:** Synchronistic events become more common during the ascension process and are a sign that things are starting to align in your life.
- **Life overhaul:** As your energy ascends you may feel the desire to radically change your life in a more positive direction. This could result in positive life changes such as a new job or relationship.
- **Feeling out of place or like an outsider:** As you ascend you may start to feel removed or separated from the world that you once knew. This is a common feeling and will pass once you begin to feel more comfortable at this new level of vibration.

- **Intense feelings of wanting to go "home":** As you advance in your ascension process it is common to feel a greater connection to source energy and a desire to return to your roots or "home."

If any of these signs of ascension are arising for you, just allow yourself to sit with them and accept them. Often ascension signs only become a problem when there is some resistance to them. Observe to see if you are resisting any changes or a new wave of positive energy is getting ready to enter into your life.

POSITIVE THOUGHTS, POSITIVE WORDS, POSITIVE ACTIONS

When positive energy begins flowing through you, it allows you to embrace positive thinking, which then allows you to speak more positively about yourself and others, which then allows you to take more positive actions in your life. In many ways the positivity is like a snowball effect. When you can program your mind to see the good in everything and focus on the positive, external situations or events will become a lot easier for you to manage and you will become clearer about the best action to take. When you speak positively about yourself and others, you also align yourself with a higher vibration. Doing so can also allow other people to focus on the positive.

What you say about others is really a reflection of how you feel about yourself:

- If you have low self-esteem, it is going to be a lot easier for you to put down someone else for looking differently or acting in a different way. This negativity is a reflection of how you would feel if you were acting differently or doing something in a different way.

- If you embrace all people and celebrate differences, you will have no reason to judge people. When we judge other people, it is because we judge ourselves harshly and feel it necessary to view other people in the same way. In fact, what we judge in others we are really just judging in ourselves.

Your words carry a powerful vibration, so what you send out into the world through your voice is either adding to the raising of consciousness of the planet or not. When you speak lovingly about yourself and other people, it allows the energy around you to be lifted up, and it also allows you to view people and yourself through the lens of compassion.

We are all just doing the best we can here on this journey, and when we keep this in mind it makes it a lot easier for us to forgive and to appreciate other people for who they are. When you practice thinking positively and speaking positively, your actions also naturally follow. When you are filled with positive energy, it becomes impossible for you to take actions that are going to harm you or others. When you are filled with positive energy, you will also begin naturally doing things that support the health and well-being of your body. It will be so natural and easy for you to eat foods that support and nourish your body and make you feel good. It will feel natural for you to exercise and take care of yourself. It will feel natural for you to look after yourself and give yourself exactly what it is that you need. When you are filled up with positive energy, your entire life takes on this shape and changes things so that you experience a whole new way of living.

CHAPTER WRAP-UP

When positive energy starts to flow through your life, you may experience a drastic shift that enhances everything to a new level. This place of being is filled with grace and ease, and it will help you to create an inspired life.

- Positive energy is a powerful force that can help to shift your life to a whole new level.
- You deserve to live a positive life and you deserve to create a life that feels good from the inside out.
- Being happy is something that you create on the inside. No external event or object can bring you true or lasting happiness.
- Don't worry about being anything other than yourself. Just be true to yourself and the rest will fall into place.
- Expectations don't always serve us. Perhaps you can find a way to release expectations that are making you feel disappointed or that are blocking you from being open to the opportunities that the Universe is bringing your way.
- Ascension signs and symptoms may become present in your life as you start shifting. They are simply part of the process and the less you resist the process, the less you will notice them.

FINAL THOUGHTS

It starts with you.

If you want to change your life and feel positive and radiant in every moment, you need to take control. Only you are responsible for your life and only you know what you need. When you start to view life as an amazing adventure, when you start to view life as a small section in a much bigger picture, you will be able to shift your mindset and the way that you view things. When you take life seriously and get wrapped up in all the chaos and mess around you, it will be impossible to live a life of alignment. When you take the stance of being an observer, when you shift out of the chaos and into your true self, you give yourself the ability to look at your life from a place of calmness and ease. This not only makes your life easier but it also makes your life more enjoyable and more fun.

We have all been given wonderful lives, but it is up to us to make it what we want to make it. Make no mistake, life is definitely a balance of moving in and out of alignment and experiencing both the darkness and the light. But once you have a taste of alignment and light, once you begin to do your best to operate from this place as frequently as possible, you will start to unravel a whole new meaning to your life. Life will feel easier, life will feel more flowing, and you will feel more connected to your purpose and to the world around you. We need suffering and pain to some extent to help us grow and develop, but if we can keep this in mind as the highest intention of our suffering, then we can see things with a newfound clarity, grace, and ease.

Life is not as serious as many of us make it out to be—it is a temporary journey of discovery, learning, growing, and enjoying. If you can step out of the seriousness and the confusion and the pain for just a moment, you will see that there is a whole world of opportunities waiting before you.

INDEX